"Priests should welcome this volume not only for their own personal growth during Lent but as a valuable source for daily lenten homilies. *40 Days of Grace* is a significant and practical volume of fresh ideas for Lent, 1996 and beyond. "

Msgr. Charles Dollen
Book Review Editor, *The Priest*

"It is a pleasure to welcome this spiritually enriching volume of lenten reflections. It weds the everyday with the profoundly spiritual in a combination that is lively and appropriate to the season."

Dr. Eugene J. Fisher
Secretariat for Ecumenical and Interreligious Affairs

"Father Wenig has again turned his poetic sense of the biblical text to a church season. His experience in Jerusalem and in rural parishes helps him to write in a way that responds vividly to our hunger to know the Bible better and to pray it more deeply."

Rev. Gordon F. Davies
St. Augustine's Seminary, Toronto

"If you need a lenten retreat this year, look no further. Fr. Laurin Wenig follows his volume of Advent reflections with this new treasure of prayer and reflection. Combining a profound understanding of the scriptures with pastoral sensitivity toward the liturgical year, these meditations will both comfort and challenge the reader. Fr. Wenig's love of the Holy Land brings the scriptural texts of the individual days of Lent to life."

Fr. Michael Witczak
St. Francis Seminary, Milwaukee

"Father Wenig is a superb Scripture scholar who explains the lenten readings so that they become compelling guides for growing in faith. He puts the Lectionary passages into context and helps us get into the minds of the biblical personages. Praying his prayers and using his reflections will go a long way toward making Lent the powerful spiritual experience God means it to be."

John Burke, O.P., S.T.D.
Director, The National Institute for the Word of God

FORTY DAYS of GRACE

LENTEN PRAYERS AND REFLECTIONS

LAURIN J. WENIG

TWENTY-THIRD PUBLICATIONS

Mystic, Connecticut 06355

Acknowledgment

Special thanks to the *Catholic Herald*, the weekly newspaper of the Archdiocese of Milwaukee, for originally publishing these reflections, which were later edited for a broader readership.

Twenty-Third Publications
185 Willow Street
P.O. Box 180
Mystic, CT 06355
(203) 536-2611
800-321-0411

ISBN 0-89622-665-4
Library of Congress Catalog Card Number 95-61145
Printed in the U.S.A.

Dedication

In gratitude to
Archbishop Rembert G. Weakland, OSB
and Bishop Richard J. Sklba
of Milwaukee
for Word and Witness
to the Risen Lord.

Contents

How to Use This Book

Lent is a rather straightforward season. The date for Ash Wednesday varies from year to year, depending upon the date of Easter. Most parishes publish a church calendar that you can use to determine when Ash Wednesday falls on any given year. All the reader has to do is to find out that beginning date, and then proceed with this book day after day throughout Lent.

Three reflections are provided for each Sunday. The following list indicates which liturgical year (A, B, or C) of the three-year cycle of the Lectionary is the appropriate one for that year.

1996	Year A	1999	Year A
1997	Year B	2000	Year B
1998	Year C	2001	Year C

I suggest that the reader find a set quiet time each day to use the reflections for each day of Lent in this book. In addition, you will also need a Bible. Begin by reading the Scripture passages assigned for each day, which are listed at the beginning of each reflection. Ponder them a bit, and then continue with the reflection provided for that day. You might then take a few extra moments to see how the reflection might apply in a special way to your life, your family, or your parish. You might use the questions after each Sunday's reflection to help you apply the reflections provided for the week to your daily life. Finally, pray the prayer provided for the day, Monday to Saturday, or let your heart speak freely to God, or listen in reverent silence.

INTRODUCTION TO LENT

Lent. Our special season, that season of the church year that every Catholic remembers. Some remember the strict fasts of years gone by; some remember giving up candy; for others, it is a time of special devotions and purple cloth covering the statues in church.

What does Lent mean? It comes from the Old English word *lencten*, "spring." The term derives from the word for lengthen, referring to the lengthening of the daylight hours, which describes spring in the northern hemisphere. That's an appropriate way to think about this season—spring. No matter the date it begins, it is winter. The trees around us are bare. They look dead, but underneath the ground and inside they are very much alive. Spring brings them to full life. That is what Lent tries to do for our souls, to bring us back to full life.

In Latin and Italian the word for Lent is the term for "40," reflecting the 40 weekdays of observance between Ash Wednesday and the Triduum, or "three days" (Holy Thursday, Good Friday, and Holy Saturday). In German, the word for Lent means "fasting time," which is what we do during that liturgical season.

This season of Lent, shared by all Christians, is very old. From the earliest times, the Christian church felt the need to prepare in a special way for Easter. By the year 325, the Council of Nicea talks about a period of preparation that would last 40 days and would be observed in one form or another throughout the Christian world.

For those who read the Bible, the number 40 recalls several great moments in faith: the flood of Noah lasted 40 days; the wandering of the Hebrews in the desert lasted 40 years; Jesus himself fasted in the wilderness of Judea for 40 days. This amount of time—40 days or 40 years—is clearly special. For the survivors of the flood, it was enough time to purify the earth. For the Hebrews, the years of desert wandering were enough time to change a group of riff-raff escaped slaves into a people of God. Even for Jesus, 40 days was enough to change him from the private person of Nazareth to a public proclaimer of the kingdom of God. Forty days or forty years seem sufficient to accomplish something worthwhile.

What do we seek to accomplish by the observance of Lent? In essence, it is to become the people God wants us to be. Lent, you see, is not just a private exercise, but a public observance of the whole church. That is why we all leave the church with ashes on our foreheads. Lent is the great annual retreat of the church, the people of God, reminding ourselves of the dignity and obligations that are ours because we are baptized.

During Lent, in many parishes, those people wishing to become Catholics or those who want to be baptized (catechumens) are presented to the community in preparation for the Easter Vigil ceremonies when they will be baptized. Lent is their period of initiation. For the rest of us, it is a time when we prepare ourselves for the great annual renewal of our own baptism with water and fire and promises. It is God who is at work in us, changing us, transforming us. Sometimes we resist change, but the Bible is clear: God continually calls each of us to become a new person "in Christ."

The great pillars of Lent are fasting, prayer, and almsgiving. These three complement one another and work together to pull us away from ungodly influences and to strengthen and guide us back to new life in Jesus.

Fasting. The fasting is not just the "giving up candy" of our childhood. There are so many ways we can fast: not just dieting, but getting healthier. Not just doing without, but also coming to understand the constant suffering of those who do not choose to fast but simply have no food. In a world that tells us we should indulge ourselves, fasting tells us something different. To fast from selfishness and ornery-ness, that too is needed!

Prayer. For many, Lent is a time of going to church a little more often: extra devotions, extra Masses. But it should also be turning us toward frequent prayer, a life of prayer, for ourselves and for others. It means using time in more godly ways than we usually do.

Almsgiving. The prophets whose words will come at us and perhaps disturb us throughout Lent are all very clear: all the prayer in the world and all the fasting imaginable are worthless unless they turn our hearts toward our neighbors. That is no easy task.

All three are necessary. All three, practiced faithfully, will lead us back to Jesus, the Risen Lord of Easter. It is usually easy to make great promises and have wonderful intentions, like New Year's resolutions. It is better to start small, to search for some one new or extra way for fasting, for prayer, and for almsgiving that we can work at faithfully day after day for 40 days.

May this book of reflections help you to understand a little better the call of God's Word. May Lent be a day-by-day grace that opens up God's love for you and your love for others. Then you will be able to look back at Lent and back at yourself and see how God has helped you to grow in faith, hope, and love.

Happy, holy Lent.

Ash Wednesday

Joel 2:12–18 • Psalm 51 • 2 Corinthians 5:20–6:2
Matthew 6:1–6,16–18

"Remember, you are dust and to dust you shall return."

When was the last time you heard that statement? Did you ever hear it? Now, on Ash Wednesday, we often hear something different when ashes are placed on our foreheads: "Reform your lives and believe in the gospel."

Both statements are true. Both are helpful. Today, though, we focus on the second sentence: not because it is any better or any more true, but because it is true and because we never hear it any more. We really don't want to hear: "Remember, you are dust and to dust you shall return."

There are many reasons we don't want to hear it. One reason is its sobering reminder that this life is not eternal. Only baptismal life is. We dread our own mortality. Another reason we don't like hearing it is the same reason why our churches are not full every Sunday. The words of the world—all those other influences out there that determine how we think, what we buy, the way we dress, and ultimately who we are—don't want us to know that we are dust. That we are limited, imperfect creatures. The world wants us to think that we are incredibly beautiful, unbelievably wise, and enviably well-dressed. Such thinking abhors this reality: we are dust.

Believers know that our souls get dusty from lack of exercise and that our lives get messy because of Adam and Eve. We follow their example and we make ourselves the measure of what is good, or right or beautiful or acceptable. The truth is: we need these words. We need Ash Wednesday. "Remember, you are dust and to dust you shall return."

Make no mistake, though. This does not mean that we are

4

unimportant or that any one of us is insignificant. The opposite is true, but not for the reason the world offers. The reason, the only reason, is this: we are made in the image and likeness of the ineffable, immortal, all-knowing, all-loving Creator, our God.

This God, the Bible tells us, is a jealous God who wants people to be close. Thus, we have Lent, calling us home, calling us back to baptism, calling us back to our own souls and to God's ways.

If we have ever found ourselves puzzled, lost, hurting, in strange situations or in front of strange gods who do not love us but want to hurt or to use us, or to abuse us, then we need the ashes.

There is something ironic about this ceremony, about Lent. We begin by placing ashes on ourselves, a visible dirt, a sign of the sin within. We end Lent in the waters of baptism, washing off the ashes, making us clean again, a sign of the new holiness within.

These ashes are a public sign, visible to all. Less public are the changes that take place within us, the forty days of daily growing in faith and coming home to God. The ashes remind us of painful truths that the world tries to laugh away or to spend away. Only God drives sin away. Through Jesus. Through the cross.

We are dust. We are also the image and likeness of God. This day, with dirt on our faces, we leave our churches in the company of our neighbors who are just like us. In forty days we will return. Our faces will be clean. A little soap and water takes care of that. That is easy. More difficult is the challenge of Lent: to purify our souls and to come home to God. Happy, holy Lent.

Lord God, at the beginning it is so easy to make promises, to think of ways to make sacrifices and so many things to do. On this first day of Lent, give me the strength to follow through and to follow your Son into the desert. Help me to see the temptations and the dirt that are part of me. Help me to exercise my soul, to become stronger in faith, in hope, and in love. Help me to come to Easter ready to renew my baptism. Amen.

Thursday After Ash Wednesday

Deuteronomy 30:15–20 • Psalm 1 • Luke 9:22–25

"Take up the cross each day."

Only one day has passed since the ashes were placed on our foreheads. Only one day and already we hear about the cross. The cross appears early in Lent and will continue to weave in and out of all our lenten readings, our meditations and practices—not to mention our lives! Like yesterday's ashes, we prefer not to deal with crosses.

One of the lessons that we all learn, sometimes all too soon, is that everyone carries some kind of cross. In a few circumstances the crosses are visible and known to everyone. More common, however, are the invisible crosses that people carry and only occasionally reveal to another. Everyone has some special burden that is part of life: an unhappy marriage, a wandering child, a quiet disease. It might be some unfulfilled dream or some old hurt that has paralyzed the energy needed to get on with life. So many, many crosses.

Jesus knew about crosses too. There was, of course, the cross of Good Friday, but there were many others besides. There was the cross of scribes and elders and high priests who would not cooperate with his plan of goodness. There were uncomprehending disciples and traitor friends.

What makes Jesus different from us is that he understood crosses from the beginning. He saw them for what they are: not punishments from God but opportunities for grace.

Everyone responds differently to burdens. Some try to shuck the cross along the wayside. Others try to throw it onto someone else's shoulders. A few, says Jesus, come to understand the mystery, that carrying your own cross and taking someone else's burden in addition actually lighten the load.

Those who run from their crosses lose all. Whoever accepts God's gift of the cross comes to share in the life of the kingdom.

Jesus must have studied the Scriptures well, for we see many similarities between his words and the words of Moses from the first reading. For some of the Israelites the commandments, statutes, and decrees of God were a burden, better ignored in favor of less demanding gods. The wise person, however, could see that these commandments were a source of joy. In truth, they were and are a way to God. The wise person chooses them and in the process chooses life.

Choosing to carry crosses has always seemed to lead only to suffering and death. Jesus changed all that; Good Friday changed all that. At beginning of this Lent we are given a choice too: to let the next forty days pass uneventfully, forgetting about yesterday's ashes and good intentions—or to walk for forty days with Jesus and to share his cross and our crosses with one another.

Lord God, it is still early in Lent. Help me to be faithful to my lenten promises. Let me see the crosses of others more clearly and to stop worrying so much about my own. Help me, most of all during these early days of Lent, to focus on your word and the way it can help me grow in holiness. Amen.

Friday After Ash Wednesday

Isaiah 58:1–9 • Psalm 51 • Matthew 9:14–15

"Is this the nature of fasting I wish?"

Accepting Lent. That's what yesterday's readings demanded from us. Today, only the second day after Ash Wednesday, the readings remind us of another of Lent's special messages: the need for and nature of fasting.

Our church shows a bit of wise humor in these reminders. Human nature is quick to make resolutions and equally quick to forget them. Our fine intentions, begun on Ash Wednesday, are put to the test early. Friday's fasting and abstaining are not as easily done as we would wish!

When we get hungry, most of us become irritable. Think of any trip when the driver doesn't stop soon enough for a meal, or when the flight attendant seems to take forever to bring the food trays around. Pilgrim people, the Bible tells us, have always been a bit on the crabby side! Travel isn't easy, whether to a vacation destination or to the kingdom of God! Is this the nature of fasting that God wishes? Irritated living? Watching the clock until we can eat what we want again? Taking our fasting out on one another?

The prophet Isaiah understood this. Capturing the all too human spirit of our fasting—"Your fast ends in quarreling and fighting!"—he summons us to remember the spirit of fasting. Lent is not just a time for dieting. Although dieting and fasting may conclude with the same result, the motivation is completely different.

Our fasting is more than just a matter of not eating. Isaiah tells us that fasting should lead us to look at ourselves differently, not just at a thinner self in the mirror, but at a renewed self. In fact, he insists that true fasting isn't a matter of calories or mirrors at all, but a matter of looking at the excesses of our own lives and at the needs of our neighbors.

Our closets are stuffed with unworn clothing. Our cupboards are filled with cans of food. Our hearts hold on to grudges, though we can be generous with complaints and gossip. Isaiah says it better: Share your bread with the hungry; shelter the oppressed and the homeless; clothe the naked when you see them; remove from your midst oppression, false accusation, and malicious speech.

As we begin to make inroads in the spirit and practice of Lent, these words serve as a worthy guide for our efforts. The gospel tells us why: if we feel the absence of Jesus in our lives, we need to fast. We need to do this until he is fully present and that will happen when we spend a Lent faithfully praying, fasting, and doing charity. This is the manner of fasting that God wishes!

Then the fasting can end not only because Easter is finally here, but because we have seen the presence of Jesus in the messianic banquet, a rich feast of his redemption, grace, and love.

Lord God, what a strange time Lent is! Although it rolls around each year, it makes demands that are always difficult and challenging. At first I like it, but then it becomes difficult. Today you ask that I begin to "give up" not just food and drink and meat, but all those habits that separate me from you and from others. Help me today to see my own excesses and my neighbors' needs. Give me the integrity I need to be faithful. Amen.

Saturday After Ash Wednesday

Isaiah 58:9–14 • Psalm 86 • Luke 5:27–32

"I have come not to call the self-righteous but sinners."

Shortly after the Christmas season our world was filled with the signs of a popular holiday, Valentine's Day. In every store the card displays reminded us to "keep this day holy." We are expected to purchase cards, flowers, and candy in order to please the love of our life and show our appreciation.

In our culture all this emotional appeal is centered in the heart; thus the red hearts dangling before us in the stores. In the Bible, the heart had quite a different function. The heart was equal to the brain, to the seat of knowledge and wisdom. (The ancients thought that emotions were located in the bowels!)

When Jesus offers his invitation to a "change of heart" he is not speaking about emotional adjustments in our lives. Rather, he is issuing a tough invitation to rethink the whole of our lives: our attitude toward God, toward neighbor, toward ourselves, and the way we spend our time and our money. For that reason, Jesus calls each of us to renewal, because it is so easy to become self-satisfied and self-righteous, to think that everyone else should change, not me.

We hear this call every Lent. At first it seems impossible to do all those things all over again, but Jesus knows well our tendency to become self-satisfied, to settle back and relax. There are times when we reach certain plateaus and deserve the chance to catch our breath, but Lent comes along to remind us that the resting cannot last forever. The temptation to remain too comfortable is always there. That was the difficulty of the Pharisees and scribes in today's gospel. They thought they had achieved the fulfillment of their religious lives and didn't need Jesus to tell them otherwise. They had the Law and they had their interpretation of that Law. For them, that was sufficient.

The twin pillars upon which Jesus rests his teaching are found in the first reading: sharing bread with those who are hungry, not only table bread but also the bread of fellowship, and proper praise of God, hallowing the Sabbath. Both God and neighbor need our attention. We all need to continue to seek new ways to accomplish these goals and to look more deeply into ourselves to search out and weed out the self-righteousness that lurks within. Again, we return to the theme of this gospel and of the day: Jesus is always directing his words at us, not at someone else. Our tendency to expect others to change is misdirected. Jesus addresses us: I have come to call sinners. That's us!

It is still early in Lent. Our readings invite us to acknowledge that our self-righteous tendencies need to be changed. Jesus himself invites us to admit that we are sinners, that we need him, and that we need to listen carefully and hear him say to us, "Follow me!"

Lord God, how much I need this gospel! How much I need your word as a true mirror for my life. Change of heart is so difficult, but so necessary. Help me to be honest with you and with myself today, to search out those parts of my life that need the healing of your love and the deeper presence of my Savior. Amen.

First Week of Lent

Each year, this Sunday of Lent leads us into the desert. Normally that would be a frightful experience, because the desert is the place of bandits and wild animals. It is the place where no law protects the hapless wanderer. It is "the pace of noises." But the desert is the proper place to begin Lent, since this is where God usually finds us: wandering, a little weary of life, a little empty of spirit, just as the desert is empty of food. The desert dryness matches our spiritual dryness, a soul often worn down and needing refreshment.

So, into the desert we go. We don't have to be afraid to go into the desert; we are in good company there. The author of Psalm 63 went there before us. "O God, you are my God whom I seek; for you my flesh pines and my souls thirsts like the earth, parched, lifeless and without water." The truth is, our soul's need for God is the same as our neighbor's need.

There is another reason to go into the desert at the beginning of Lent: Jesus went there. We need never be afraid to go wherever Jesus went before us, into deserts or into death. He always calms our fears and tells us that it is all right—all right to go into Lent's desert to search our souls and to find out what kind of refreshment we need in order to come to the life-giving water of the Easter Vigil.

Some practical ways to begin the lenten journey might be to make a list of those parts of our lives that don't seem right just now, the things that bother us. They might include problems at home or work or school. It might include the ways we forget God or the relationships in our life that are shaky. It often helps to see all these problem areas in front of us and then decide which most need God's grace—and our efforts.

Something else is needed too. In the desert there is time

to look for God. There is nothing to distract us. Make the commitment this first Sunday of Lent to set aside some special "desert time" for yourself each day, a time to read these reflections, a time to pray, a time to be by yourself. Look into the special lenten programs that might be offered in your parish, neighborhood, or city. Resolve to let others into your Lent by taking advantage of the programs of talks, days of reflection, devotions, and prayer that are available.

Finally, forgive yourself! This first week of Lent is full of temptation to backslide. Perhaps all the good intentions of Ash Wednesday have already been broken. Forgive yourself and start over. That's what Lent is all about: starting over with God.

First Sunday of Lent
Year A

Genesis 2:7–9,3:1–7 • Romans 5:12–19
Matthew 4:1–11

It is proper that Lent begins in a garden. No ordinary garden, it is the Garden of Eden, the first garden. Genesis teaches that God planted this garden and as one might expect of a garden planted by God, it was "delightful to look at and good for food." Lent will end in another garden, the rock-tomb garden where Jesus will rise from the dead in glory. How will we use these 40 days to travel from garden to garden, from sin to redemption, from death to life?

But first, this other garden. "What in the world went wrong there?" people have asked since the beginning. "Why do we fear God?" "Why do we fear each other?" "What is it within us that causes relationships to fall apart: between men and women, between husbands and wives, between children and parents, between brothers and sisters, between blacks and whites, between Jews and Muslims, and on and on and on?"

To answer such questions we point to this story and its rather uncomfortable lesson: it has always been that way. What should have been the ideal human relationship soon disintegrated. Paradise was lost.

If you read the story carefully you might catch part of the problem. While chatting with the serpent about God's prohibitions, Eve adds one: "You shall not even touch the tree, lest you die." But God never said that. The rabbis of old taught that right here we should learn a lesson: embroidering the truth is the opening that sin needs to find its way into our lives.

Genesis says that Adam and Eve "had their eyes opened." They saw themselves for what they really were. They were not pleased with what they saw. They had been tempted and they fell from grace. What appeared to be good wasn't good. Isn't that the same lesson we keep learning the hard way? At the beginning of Lent we too look at ourselves, and what do we see? This simple Genesis story exposes our sinfulness too. We desire more than we have and more than we need. We make bad decisions. We mess life up, for ourselves and for others. We too fall from grace.

The gospel points us to another place, the desert. This is no garden. Here ancient Israel was tempted. Here, ancient Israel made bad decisions. The response to God's incredible redemption from Egypt was nothing but complaints! Sounds familiar, doesn't it? In the desert God made a covenant, a solemn agreement, with the Israelites. Moses would keep reminding them not to abandon the covenant. He would call them to be faithful, a fidelity that is marked by listening to God's word and doing it. We call this obedience, another uncomfortable word.

Jesus was tempted in the desert. Even Jesus, the Son of God, was tempted to make bad decisions, to benefit himself rather than obey God. In the garden the first son and daughter of humanity failed. In the desert the sons and daughters of Israel failed. This son will not fail.

Temptation wears many disguises. Once it slithered into human life as a serpent. It continues to come in subtle, crafty ways. It comes to each of us in a special guise, ready to work on our weakness. What is that weakness? Where do each of us most need God to make us strong? That's the question that this first Sunday of Lent poses. Before Lent can work for us, we have to go to the garden and to the desert and take time for ourselves to admit we need redemption, to admit we are sinners, to acknowledge we are the children of Adam and Eve.

Our lenten journey takes us back to that first garden and its sin. It also takes us to the other garden, to the place where Christ's obedience broke sin's power over our world and over

16

our lives. St. Paul said it so well in the second reading: "For if by the offense of the one man all died, much more did the grace of God and the gracious gift of the one man, Jesus Christ, abound for all."

The sad truth is, we more often imitate Adam than we do Jesus. The good news is another Lent, another chance to renew our baptism and to journey with Jesus and learn from him how to be faithful and then to renew our baptismal bonds at Easter.

Questions for Reflection

1. What lenten practice can help you discipline the temptations that confront you?

2. What local lenten program is being offered for your spiritual growth? Will you participate in it?

3. Jesus was tempted to misuse his power for self-serving purposes. This Lent, how can you use your time and gifts to serve others in a special way?

First Sunday of Lent
Year B

Genesis 9:8–15 • 1 Peter 3:18–22 • Mark 1:12–15

One of the words we heard about when we were growing up was "sin." How many times did we hear, "Don't do that. That's a sin"? Or "Avoid sin—do good!" We know that people sin; we know that we sin. We hurt people and they hurt us. If everyone were to write down a definition of sin there would be a lot of words dealing with good and evil, something we spend a lot of time and energy grappling with.

The gospel on this first Sunday of Lent tells us that Jesus wrestled with these problems too. Like us, he was tempted. The Old Testament, the book that taught Jesus, speaks a lot about sin. The people who occupy its pages were not much different from us; they too had to wrestle with good and evil. One of the Bible's earliest authors tried to answer the question about where evil comes from. Why, in this world that has so much potential for goodness, is there so much evil?

The nameless writer of today's Genesis reading invites us to travel back to the beginning of the world, to a time when everything was "the way it should be." We know the story. Adam and Eve were a couple whose relationship was what it should be. Everything was right. Adam and Eve also lived in a proper relationship with God, who walked with them in the cool of the evening and chatted with them about the day's events.

All that goodness corroded; it turned evil and made things the way they are today. You know the story. The man blames the woman. The woman passes on the blame to the serpent who had cleverly appealed to base human instinct: to want more, to want to be like God. God was holding back from us, said the serpent, so we reached out for more. We turned our collective human back on all that we had in order to stretch for more. Then we would be happy. Soon brother was pitted against brother, neighbor against neighbor. This beautiful, good creation had turned from God. In every way, death was the result of sin.

Then came the Flood. The deluge. Here we are, at the beginning of Genesis, at the origin of human history. We have no sooner taken our first collective breath of life than we begin to see the end. The end of history. The end of humanity. From the beginning of time we have been preoccupied with the end. Why? What force is there inside us—or outside—that focuses our attention on the end of the world? Is it human destiny? Or some perversion of faith? Here, in Genesis, in these few chapters, we find these refined biblical thoughts about real and imagined, potential and actual destructions.

Woven in front of us is a marvelous tapestry of oriental mythology and biblical theology, all of it pointing to the Bible's certainty that God is good. God does not will destruction for us, despite our self-destructive tendencies. As proof, a rainbow is placed in the sky, a technicolor reminder to God of the promise never to destroy again. The same rainbow reminds us of the grace and forbearance of the Creator. It is a sacrament of the covenant God makes with us, the solemn promise to be for us, no matter what, forever. God's goodness gives second chances. New creations.

Eden's serpent will always lose. In the desert, the tempter lost to Jesus. In our own struggle with good and evil, good will win because of the graciousness of our God. We will not spend the next 40 days in an ark searching for rainbows, or in the desert avoiding the tempter. We will spend these days repairing the damage we have done to our relationships with neighbor. We will repair our broken relationships with God. Lent is our annual pilgrimage back to God, our annual promise that God's covenant and Jesus' love endure our assaults against the kingdom.

The rainbow that reminds God of his promise tugs at our Catholic consciences during these forty days. It summons us out of our routines and into the Spirit. It calls us out of the flood of life's difficulties that always threatens to overwhelm us. The rainbow invites us to let the waters of our baptism wash over us as we march toward Easter and make our way out of sin and more deeply into the life of Jesus. Hence the summons of the gospel: Reform your lives and believe in the Good News!

Questions for Reflection

1. Jesus was tempted in the desert. What three areas of your life are under assault and need God's grace this Lent?

2. What "plan of action" can you take to assist in helping yourself to "reform your life" in these areas?

3. What problems seem to be flooding into your life now? Who can help you? How can you help yourself?

4. What lenten programs for education or prayer are available in your parish church or area this season?

First Sunday of Lent
Year C

Deuteronomy 26:4–10 • Romans 10:8–13 • Luke 4:1–13

Jebel Quruntul. That is what the Arabs in the neighborhood call this site. The Mount of Temptations. It rises out of the Jordan Valley, near Jericho. From the lowest place on the face of Earth to this high summit, that is the setting for the First Sunday of Lent this year. From this peak you can see the eternally silent shore of the Dead Sea. The Copper Scroll, one of the Dead Sea Scrolls, tells of buried treasure on this mountain. The Mount of Olives can be seen from here. So can the entire Judean wilderness and another mountain, Nebo, where Moses is buried. It takes a healthy hiker over an hour to climb to the summit. Once there, it seems you can see all the kingdoms of the world.

The Crusaders were the first to consider this site as the location for this gospel. On the slope of the hill a Greek Orthodox monastery hangs on the rockface, a perennial reminder of the precarious nature of our survival in this world, indeed of our survival without God. Near the foot of this rock, the Jordan River lazes its way into the Dead Sea. To this day the fountain of Elisha splashes water into the irrigation canals of Jericho. But to one who goes out into the wilderness, the water is far away. So too is food. And sound. That's why people went out into the desert: to get away from the noise of the world and to listen to their souls. To listen to God.

We meet Jesus in this desert. No food. No water. No voice. The setting is quietly haunting. Other than the rustling of the wind through the treeless heights, there is no sound. Jesus is alone. He is hungry. He is vulnerable. Aren't we all, no matter where we are?

Why would anyone go out to such a place? Why take such

risks? No one can do it on a personal initiative. Even here, it's the Holy Spirit that prompts Jesus.

In that desert Jesus squares off with God's competition, with the devil, that master tempter, the father of lies. Like Eve in the garden, the temptations do not come from within, but are clearly the responsibility of something else, of someone else. "The devil made me do it," we say. But Jesus conquers the devil. Jesus conquers all evil.

The contest of wills between Jesus and the devil is a struggle for fidelity. Many years before this event, Israel wandered in the desert. There, this favored people was tempted to deny their identity and their destiny. The quotations from Deuteronomy are reminders of those difficult years when Israel was searching for a proper relationship with God. Israel was put to the test in the desert and failed. Jesus will be put to the test, but he doesn't fail. Because of him, we needn't fail either.

It is a question of discipleship and vocation. Israel was called to be dependent upon God, but Israel sought food apart from God. In the desert Israel gave in to the worship of golden calves, other gods; in the desert Israel tested God's patience (Deuteronomy 8:3; 6:13; 6:16). When the Hebrews faced forces of hostility and opposition in the desert, they yielded and they lost. Deuteronomy was written so that this people would never forget its precarious origins. But our Jesus did not yield when he was in the desert; he remained faithful to his call, to his identity and mission. This gospel tells us that with Jesus we too can conquer temptation. If Jesus had to struggle with temptation, who can be exempt from it?

It is Lent, time for our annual pilgrimage into ourselves and outward toward others. God's Spirit leads us into the desert of Lent for our own 40-day struggle with ourselves. It is time for our annual examination of conscience, to look at ourselves and see where our own social, personal, and religious lives are heading. It is a time to think, a time to act and to pray. Are we being faithful to our own mission to live the gospel and to our own identity as Christian? If not, why not? Lent is a time to recapture the vitality of our baptism. It begins with this gospel, in the desert. It will end in Jerusalem on Easter Sunday. Happy, holy Lent!

Questions for Reflection

1. What temptations did Jesus face? How are they like our own?

2. What kind of desert do you seem to be wandering in? What source of refreshment or grace do you need this Lent?

3. Israel was tempted to abandon its vocation to be God's people. How have you abandoned your baptism? How has your parish abandoned its mission? What can you do about it this Lent?

4. What real, practical changes do you want to make this Lent? Write them down and check them each Sunday.

5. Lent moves inward and outward. What inward practices of religion do you need to rediscover this Lent? What outward charity and activities toward others do you or your parish need to energize this Lent?

Monday of the First Week

Leviticus 19:1–2,11–18 • Psalm 19 • Matthew 25:31–46

"Be holy as I am holy!"

This is no small commandment. The beginning and the end of this reading from Leviticus address the holiness of God. If you look at this passage in the Bible or in the Lectionary, you will notice that between the first and last commandments there are many other duties that describe how to achieve this holiness. But nowhere in that instruction does it mention what you might expect to find! God does not tell us to go to church or to the synagogue or to the mosque—or even to pray! Instead, there is a long list of duties toward our neighbor, an outline of decent, human behavior that is a truer reflection of the holiness God wants.

Isn't that one of the goals of Lent, to renew our baptismal commitment and become holy? Because God's concern for us is that we become holy, no one less than God offers an outline of how we can achieve it. These sentences repeat and deepen the Ten Commandments, those that deal with our neighbor.

In the gospel Jesus shows that he has absorbed this same trait from God, his Father. Observe that the judgment scene about the end of the world says nothing about prayer or halos or any of the usual matters we tend to associate with God. Jesus knows his religion well; he understands perfectly and teaches us clearly that our true self is revealed by the way we think about our neighbor and treat our neighbor, not by lip service to God. To become holy means to be what God is: holy, which means that we do what God does: take care of others.

The prophet known as "Second Isaiah" was the most poetic of Israel's prophets. He writes about the image of God and how it is found in all people, not just those we like, not just our fellow believers or compatriots. Jesus repeats this "performance principle," and those who truly grasp his message will seek to imitate him. This gospel reverberates with an instruction about our lenten custom of almsgiving, of caring for those who need our help.

All the prayer and fasting we might do count for naught unless we open our eyes to see Jesus in others. "Be holy as I am holy!" Indeed, that is a challenge worthy of Lent!

Lord God, open my eyes today to see you in my neighbor. In all my neighbors. Open my eyes to see the way you use others to help me grow in faith. Let me hear their words of need. Let me see their good deeds toward me. Let me use my hands to reach out and to do good, not for the sake of reward, but because it is the right thing to do. May my almsgiving in all its forms bring me closer to you. Amen.

Tuesday of the First Week

Isaiah 55:10–11 • Psalm 34 • Matthew 6:7–15

"This is how you are to pray."

Our annual observance of Lent rests on three pillars: prayer, fasting, and almsgiving. In the first several days of Lent our daily readings have encouraged us in the practices of fasting without becoming crabby and of seeing the genuine needs of our neighbors and responding to them with spontaneous kindness.

Today the weekday reading for Lent reminds us of the first pillar: prayer. The dictionary reminds us that "prayer" is derived from a Latin word meaning "to beg." It can also mean to communicate with a deity. Every religion has its special forms of prayer. For example, a Muslim stops all activity five times a day, kneels toward Mecca, and prays to Allah.

How should we pray? In this gospel, Jesus instructs us on how his disciples ought to pray. The words of Jesus in this segment of Matthew's gospel are well known: the "Our Father," the "Lord's Prayer." Less well known are his words leading up to this well known prayer. Often people will comment that they have "prayed and prayed" and "said all kinds of prayers," yet God doesn't seem to respond.

Jesus insists that merely reciting formulas or trying to impress God with many words isn't what really matters. He is very much concerned with how we pray, not just the right words, but the right idea behind our words. What matters is the attitude we bring to prayer. Absolute trust in God's will, mysterious and puzzling as that may be, is essential. As Isaiah says, "God's word will achieve the purpose for which it was sent." That kind of confidence should characterize the way we pray. How and when God "answers" our prayer will surprise us.

Likewise, Jesus uniquely insists that forgiveness of others is a precondition to prayer. The forgiveness we seek from God is returned in the same measure that we offer forgiveness to others!

"This is how you are to pray." During Lent we ought to observe the admonition of Jesus: keep your prayer simple and honest. Trust that God's will for us is more loving and more generous than we can ever imagine.

Lord God, teach me to pray simply this Lent. From the heart. Many words are not necessary. Nor are memorized words. My own honest speaking with you is what matters most. Help me to take time out of my day just for you, a special, sacred time to get to know you and your will and your love. Amen.

Wednesday of the First Week

Jonah 3:1–10 • Psalm 51 • Luke 11:29–32

"No sign will be given but the sign of Jonah."

One week has passed since ashes were crossed on our foreheads, a sign of an important season in our church and a sign of our voluntary participation in the discipline of Lent. For one week we have been fasting and praying, and focusing on doing more for others. How appropriate that on this day, one week since we received ashes, the readings remind us of our need to repent, to change our lives because we are taking God's word into our lives in deeper measure.

The prophet Jonah commands sackcloth and ashes, ancient signs of sorrow. It is a familiar story, this one. We all know about Jonah and the great fish. Fewer people, though, know the end of the story. Poor Jonah. He is the tragic character that lurks somewhere inside each of us. He is afraid of God, of people, of himself. He tries to run away from God, but that is impossible. We know that but perhaps Jonah didn't. Or if he did, he didn't really want to believe it. At any rate, he was a poor sign. God asked Jonah to do something very difficult, to go to a foreign land and preach repentance. God can also call us to very difficult tasks. Sometimes it just seems to be too much for us, and so we try to run, as Jonah did. We, too, become bad signs.

Jonah failed. The sailors didn't like him. Even the great fish didn't like him, so it spat him out. Jonah learned the hard way that there is no escaping God. For our part, we have to learn that there is no escaping the water of our baptism. Unlike the sign of Jonah, it is a sign that lasts.

When Jonah finally accepted that truth, he went to the great city of Nineveh, a hated enemy of his people. He wanted to have Nineveh destroyed, yet his duty was to try to save it. He preached God's word to the people there, to a people least likely to listen to it. Prophets had been sent to Israel for hundreds of years, great prophets like Isaiah and Jeremiah. The Bible records the sad truth: hardly anyone listened. Even the animals repented. Now, when a whiney, unlikeable fellow like Jonah is sent to a foreign place to preach the word of Israel's God, everyone listens. He is incredibly successful!

Jesus knew this story too. He began his public preaching with the same words as Jonah and the prophets before him, "Repent! Change!" Unlike Jonah, Jesus was not very successful. People preferred old customs, their old ways. Change can be very difficult for any of us, especially when we think we have everything figured out.

Many times people look for signs that God approves of this or disapproves of that. Some folks even become superstitious about the whole thing! Jesus is clear. Don't waste your time looking to the skies for a sign. Instead, look to that most imporant word of Lent: change. One of the greatest challenges of Lent is not to keep fasting, not to multiply prayers, not to just give and give away, but to hear this single word and to take it to heart. Reform! Reshape your lives. "For at the preaching of Jonah they reformed, but you have a greater one than Jonah here"—Jesus.

Lord God, what a message! There are so many things you are trying to say to me. Help me to open my ears to your word and my heart to its meaning. Help me not to seek signs of approval, but be busy about fixing my own life. Help me trust myself more. Help me to trust my community more and to reshape my life in your image and likeness. Amen.

Thursday of the First Week

Esther C 12,14–16,23–25 • Psalm 138 • Matthew 7:7–12

Lord, on the day I called for help, you answered me.

This simple sentence is the refrain for today's psalm. It reviews a most basic teaching: Ours is a God who hears our prayers. Prayer works! Today's readings insist on that. It is appropriate that we hear this again as our lenten liturgy parades before us another of the pillars of Lent: prayer. Earlier this week we reflected on the gospel passage in which Jesus teaches us the Our Father and reminds us to make our prayers simple and trusting. Today God reminds us that the time, effort, and faith we put into our prayer are worthwhile.

It almost seems strange to have to repeat something like that, doesn't it? Yet, our experience shows that prayer can become associated with superstition (if only I say the right amount of prayers in this certain way), or with disappointment (God doesn't seem to answer the way I expect). That is why we need today's readings. That is why we need the assurance that God does listen.

The first reading hearkens back to a time of terrible persecution for the Jewish people. A bold queen risks the wrath of her husband-king by daring to enter his presence uninvited— a scene worthy of a biblical movie! About to make this bold move, Esther prays with confidence to her God and ours, asking for courage and reminding herself and God of the promises God made to act for us, not against us.

Unlike the "foreign" gods which are only idols, our God listens to our prayer and is moved to respond. The Bible insists that praying makes a difference in our lives. It makes a difference to God. That is why Queen Esther could be so confident that God would hear her prayer.

Our relationships develop only if we spend time getting to know others. The same is true concerning God. If we want a relationship with God that is more than superstition or convenience, we need to spend time with God in trustful prayer.

Earlier in this Matthean gospel and earlier this week, Jesus taught his disciples about prayer. It seems they have been trying to follow Jesus' advice, but now they want to know if it is worthwhile. "Does God hear our prayer?" The answer is a confident and resounding yes! If we know how to respond to human needs with common sense and compassion, how much more will God respond with divine power and love?

Sometimes we make our theology so complicated. All the books about prayer and all the prayer books ever written cannot match the simple, straightforward advice that Jesus gives us today. If you don't ask, you cannot receive. "Lord, on the day I called for help, you answered." God is waiting to hear from us.

Lord God, I want to pray and pray well, not just to receive, but to praise you and to thank you. Help me to open my soul to you and to trust in your power and your goodness. Lord, teach me how to pray. Amen.

Friday of the First Week

Ezekiel 18:21–28 • Psalm 130 • Matthew 5:20–26

"Unless your holiness surpasses that of the scribes and Pharisees, you shall not enter the kingdom of God."

The scribes and the Pharisees receive very bad publicity in the gospels. Even dictionaries tend to define these words as synonyms for hypocrisy. The truth is that the scribes and Pharisees were more often well-respected, and deservedly so. Like any group of people, there were some who were not so praiseworthy. We tend to forget the others who were.

The scribes were the learned people, those who could read and write. Of course, this also gave them a great amount of power. An unscrupulous scribe could cheat people for his own benefit. The Pharisees were lay people who wanted to take their religion seriously. Their movement began at a time when the religious leaders of the people were less than admirable. As a movement, the teachings and actions of the Pharisees were at the heart of the Jewish religion at the time of Jesus. The heart of their teaching was being "holy." Of course, in any religion that may at times take bizarre turns or attract odd characters!

Our meditation today asks us to look at those well-intentioned and successful people, the scribes and the Pharisees. They were willing to do more than what Jewish law required in order to achieve their lofty goal. Jesus is calling his disciples and us to go beyond even that—to surpass the holiness of the scribes and Pharisees.

At the heart of his teaching in today's gospel Jesus insists on reconciliation with others. Notice again that there is nothing about spending extra hours in prayer or self-denial.

Instead, our attention is drawn to that most difficult part of our lives: developing positive relationships with others. Jesus insists that forgiveness and reconciliation are absolutely necessary in our relationships with God and others.

The first reading from the prophet Ezekiel teaches the very same truth. God does not hover about, watching and waiting for us to falter, but encourages us to do what is necessary to right the wrongs of our lives, to reconcile ourselves to God and neighbor.

The catchword for Lent is "repent." Turn your life around. About face. March back toward the path that will lead to holiness, to God, to the kingdom. Ezekiel's ancient words summon us back to God through obedience to the Scriptures. Jesus' words summon us back to God and to neighbor by putting into practice the words that so easily trip from our lips: "Forgive us our trespasses as we forgive those who trespass against us."

It's quite a task, isn't it, to make our own holiness surpass that of the scribes and the Pharisees? There's still a lot of work ahead for all us this Lent, isn't there?

Lord God, holiness seems so distant, so difficult. It seems like something for others to achieve, perhaps for full-time religious "professionals." Yet, day after day in Lent you are calling me to holiness, to live with a sense of my own baptismal dignity and call, to see your image and likeness in my neighbor. With your grace this day of Lent, may I see how I can grow in holiness, in healthy religious practice, in the way of your Son. Amen.

Saturday of the First Week

Deuteronomy 26:16–19 • Psalm 119 • Matthew 5:43–48

"In a word, you must be perfected as your heavenly Father is perfect."

What a challenge! Such a commandment! Can Jesus be serious? Perfection equal to God's own? It seems impossible, doesn't it? Almost frightening. It would be easy to dismiss it as an unachievable ideal, but we can't do that. It is always too easy to do that with God's word—explain it away, diminish its demands on us. Instead, we must dig into it a little deeper to look for its meaning and how it applies to our lives.

There is another meaning for this hard word "perfection." It is this: goal. Or this: purpose. The goal of our human living is to grow into the very holiness of God. That is the purpose of our existence as individuals and as a community: to keep developing, to continue to grow toward the purpose for which God has created each of us with our uniqueness. Don't these words of Jesus come to our ears a little easier with this understanding?

These words are from the most challenging part of Matthew's gospel, chapters 5-7, the "Sermon on the Mount." Throughout these chapters Jesus makes one message very clear. If we wish to be his disciples, we cannot allow ourselves the human luxury of "just getting by." Doing only what is necessary is not sufficient in the eyes of Jesus. Instead, searching for all we can do is a goal truly worthy of our baptism.

In this brief passage of that famous Sermon, Jesus pushes his listeners to go the extra measure, to go beyond what is necessary, even to go past what is possible. That is the only way that any of us fulfill our potential. In this gospel Jesus is like a good coach or teacher who knows the athlete or student well

---

enough to push him as far as possible. That is why he pushes us "to be perfect."

In the first reading of the day, there is a clue as to how we can do this. In the passage from Deuteronomy we read about the way to achieve the purpose that God has in mind for us: "You are to walk in his ways and observe his statutes, commandments and decrees, and to hearken to his voice." Moses gave that instruction to people who were serious about their relationship with God. In turn, to help them, God gave them the commandments.

Altogether the Old Testament records 613 commandments. Ten of them are very famous. Four of those ten deal with our relationship with God. All the others speak about our relationship with our neighbor! There is the clue that Lent keeps parading before our eyes. If we are to take Lent seriously, if we want to find the purpose of our lives and accomplish it, then we need to pay proper attention to God and to neighbor; to love one is to love the other. Does that balance exist in your life?

Lord God, it is so easy to focus only on you and to forget my neighbor. It is also easy to get caught up in the words of the law and to forget their purpose, to help me to live in justice and peace with my neighbor. Help me today to put my energy into looking again at your commandments, to see them as a help and not something to fear. Enable me to understand that the best way to approach you, my God, is through my neighbor. Amen.

SECOND WEEK OF LENT

The days of Lent pass by quickly. It is already Week Two. For some, the time has been marked with fidelity to those original lenten intentions. For others, there was perhaps some back-sliding, some slipping along the journey to Easter. That's normal, a part of the human condition. So much so, in fact, that this second week of Lent comes forward to address the reality head on.

In all three years of the liturgical cycle, the second week of Lent begins by taking us back to Genesis, back to the beginning, back to some situation of our ancestors in faith that shows how they too had to grow a great deal in faith. For them the journey was even more difficult, not because the topography of the land had yet to be tamed, but because they did not have the advantage of the roadmap we call the Bible to help them along their way. That is one reason why these daily lenten readings are so important; they have been carefully selected and arranged to help us make our way together to Easter.

In each of these three years we hear the gospel of the Transfiguration. Jesus leads three of his favorite followers up the steep slope of Mt. Tabor so that Jesus can communicate with the great religious leaders of the past, Moses and Elijah, and so that his disciples can get a rare glimpse of the true Jesus, Son of God.

The change that takes place in Jesus on that occasion was not just physical. Not just a spectacle. This episode marked the beginning of a new phase in his life, for after the ascent to the mountain he would lead his disciples on the ascent to Jerusalem where he would suffer and die. It is as though Jesus is saying to us, "You've come this far now. Walk with me a little longer in Lent. Let's finish the course."

Each Sunday in Lent gives us the opportunity to refresh ourselves for our Easter preparations. The readings offer a renewed impetus to pick up our promises wherever we left them along the wayside and to continue the journey toward Jerusalem, toward Easter.

Here are some things you might think about this week:

1. Have you found in your parish or neighborhood a special lenten program to attend?

2. Regarding prayer: What is your best time for reflection? Are you letting the season take over some of life's busy-ness?

3. Regarding fasting: How faithful have you been? Is today a good time to reward yourself for your fidelity to the fast? Have you found ways to fast from other things than food: e.g., wasting time, watching too much TV, being too busy?

4. Regarding almsgiving: Have you contributed in some way to someone in need? Is there a little pinch of sacrifice present in your life that wasn't there two weeks ago? Is there a local food pantry you can assist with donations or time? Is there a nearby nursing home that might need some assistance? Are there parish needs that you can help meet by some limited volunteer work? Have you made any efforts to reach out to someone you haven't been close to or have hurt?

Second Sunday of Lent
Year A

Genesis 12:1–4 • 2 Timothy 1:8–10 • Matthew 17:1–9

The Bible is not just some ancient story, a collection of old tales. It is also our story. The word of God lives on through time not just because it tells us about "then and there," but because it also describes us, in the "here and now." Whenever we find a passage somewhat confusing or challenging, it helps to place ourselves in the story. For example, not only Adam and Eve eat forbidden fruit; we do, too. Not only did the Israelites wander in the desert; we get lost, too. On Easter, not only Peter and John peek into the empty tomb, but so do we. We are wise if we join these ancestors of our faith in these biblical events, trying to figure out what God is doing to us and through us. When we make the effort to do this, very often we gain wonderful new insights and we begin to see life through the eyes, ears, and soul of faith.

The first reading invites us into the world of Abraham and Sarah, "our ancestors in faith." We all get a little glimpse into what that part of the world is like when news of the Middle East and the Persian Gulf are on television. The flat, dry, dusty land shows how difficult life has always been in that part of creation.

What television doesn't show is what Abraham and Sarah must have thought about God's initiative in their lives. God suddenly disrupts everything they knew and commands them to travel to a distant, strange land, a place where no one speaks their language, a place of new customs and many dangers. When God issues the command, there is no map or guide. God does give this old, childless couple a reason for going: "Do this and you will be great!" Abraham and Sarah trusted God. They did what God asked of them.

There it is, the journey of faith. Isn't that what life is? For the faithless, life is more like a competitive ladder of success to be climbed. For the faithful, it is a journey that takes us to new places in our souls. The summons for the journey begins somewhere deep inside each of us. For some, it begins with hard, nagging questions, and is often a puzzling or hurtful experience. Curiosity leads others to look at bigger worlds and to wander in and out of other people's lives, and in the process they meet God.

Whenever we travel we encounter difficulties: roadblocks, detours, accidents, and delays. In the spiritual journey to God we also encounter difficulties. We give them a name: cross. Doubt. Death. Divorce. Pain. Sickness. Sin. All of these, a cross. The cross.

If we are faithful to God's promptings and to the promise, the Abraham within us will rise up and say, "I too must make the journey." If we do this, then we too will inherit the blessing God promises.

We learn early in life that this journey cannot be made alone. Even Jesus wanted companions for the journey; Peter, James, and John accompanied him to the mountaintop, but they were not like Abraham. They wanted to stay at the mountaintop rather than to keep on traveling. It is always easier to rest and stay where you are. But that is not allowed, not for them and not for us.

On that summit, the three apostles saw something their companions did not see: the true Jesus. The transfigured Jesus. A changed Jesus. The gospel tells us that they saw the outside change. It says nothing about the inside, about seeing that part of Jesus. That takes a lifetime of discipleship.

In Lent, God asks us to undertake a transforming journey, to change. It is not enough to transform only our outside, like putting on spring clothes at Easter. The changes we are asked to make must take place deep inside, where our own true selves wait, often frightened, often tempted to stand still or to turn back.

But then Jesus comes along. He offers us Abraham as an example. He also reaches his hand out to us, as he once reached out to Peter, James, and John and says, "Get up!" That's our challenge. He also says, "Do not be afraid!" That is our comfort.

Questions for Reflection

1. As you enter the second week of Lent, what changes have you seen taking place in your life as a result of your observance of this sacred season?

2. What changes do you still want to make? What changes are you afraid of?

3. Which character of today's readings seems to describe you? Why? In what way?

4. Jesus was transfigured, changed, in the sight of three followers. How has your image and understanding of Jesus changed throughout your life? How has this happened?

Second Sunday of Lent
Year B

Genesis 22:1–2,9,10–13,15–18 • Romans 8:31–34
Mark 9:2–10

God put Abraham to the test. "Take your son, Isaac, your only one whom you love, and go to the land of Moriah. There you shall offer him up as a holocaust on a height that I will point out to you." What terrible words these are! How strange! How disturbing!

Throughout the centuries, Jewish, Christian, and Muslim theologians and teachers have tried to fathom its meaning. What can it be? Should we focus on God who tests us? Or should we place the emphasis on us, who are tested? Is this passage about the nature of faith? Or about the demands that faith makes on us? What is the key to understanding such incredible words from God?

The text clearly says that God puts Abraham to the test. It never clearly says what he is being tested for. Is it to test Abraham's faith in God's promise? Or to test Abraham's obedience? Why must God test us at all? Doesn't God know all things? Perhaps the lesson is about our willingness to sacrifice others instead of practicing self-sacrifice. So many questions about so few words!

The Talmud, that great book of Jewish learning, says that whenever this episode is read, the shofar must be sounded. The shofar is a ram's horn, just like the ram in the story that was caught in the thicket. The shofar should be blown to remember this story and to ponder its mystery, but especially to remember that God's promise to Abraham came true. God stayed the hand of Abraham before he could sacrifice his son, the son of the promise. The horn is also sounded to remind us that we must always be ready to sacrifice for the sake of God.

The Talmud also teaches that the shofar must be bent, a reminder that we are to bend our hearts, souls, and ears toward God.

Perhaps that is why we read this Genesis passage during Lent, which is when we are called to make voluntary sacrifice and to listen more attentively to God's word. Perhaps we are the ones who are bound up, and we just don't get anywhere that way. We let ourselves get tied up—wrapped up—in the silly things that we make so important. We get caught up in our own small world and our own problems. Lent is when we should straighten out our mixed-up values, when we should turn away from our selfishness, open our eyes to the needy, and reach out to them.

Then there are always those others we tie up; we want them to think our way, to do things our way, to be like us. When they don't correspond to what we think is acceptable, we dismiss them. Lent is a time to set people free and to set ourselves free from whatever is blocking our listening to God and living a life worthy of baptism.

Maybe the answer to the puzzle of this Genesis passage can be found in today's gospel. Jesus speaks about rising from the dead, the conclusion to his own sacrifice on the cross. In this passage he does not yet refer to his own impending sacrifice. Like Isaac, he does not run from it. He doesn't force it on others. Jesus carries the full burden of his sacrifice, just as he will carry the wood of his cross as Isaac carried the wood for his father, Abraham.

While the disciples were hiking up the mountainside with Jesus, they must have wondered what he was up to, just as Isaac wondered what Abraham was going to do. Isaac, James, John, and Peter all were unsuspecting partners in God's plan. So are we, privileged eavesdroppers in the conversation and experience of Jesus and his favorite disciples. Today we peek at the glory of Jesus that we will understand only at Easter.

In Genesis, God commanded Abraham to go, to sacrifice.

We fear sacrifice and resist it. In the end God did not require Abraham to sacrifice his son, yet God allowed Jesus, his son, to die on the cross. In the gospel, God commanded the disciples to listen. It is Lent. Will we obey these commands? Will we sacrifice? Will we listen, really listen?

Questions for Reflection

1. God's command to Abraham seemed beyond the realm of possibility. What "demands" does God seem to be making of you that seem beyond your ability to understand?

2. Sacrifice means to "make holy." What sacrifices have you been making this Lent?

3. Abraham and Jesus both made journeys of faith. In our own pilgrimage to God we often get lost. Is there a story from your life where your wondering or wandering took you to a difficult place you didn't intend to go?

4. God commanded the three apostles to listen to the words of Jesus. How can you improve your listening to the word of God by study? By prayer?

Second Sunday of Lent
Year C

**Genesis 15:5–12,17–18 • Philippians 3:17–4:1
Luke 9:28–36**

Our journey continues. Last week we traveled to the Mount of Temptations, near the Dead Sea. Our companions were Jesus and the devil, a small cast of two.

This gospel urges us to climb yet another mountain, Mt. Tabor. It is far from Jericho and the barren, rocky Judean wilderness. This solitary mountain raises its rounded summit out of the lush, fertile Valley of Jezreel, the breadbasket of ancient Israel. It is near Nazareth, where Jesus was reared. My guess is that he knew the place well. At Tabor, the Israelite general Barak and the woman judge Deborah defeated the enemy led by Sisera. There is a legend that Abraham met Melchizedek at a cave on this mount. Jesus must have known its wooded heights, perhaps played there as a child or picnicked there on a summer day. These days tourists travel to the peak in crowded taxis driven by the local Arabs. The potholed road that leads to the top is little more than a broken asphalt lane. Sheer drop-offs panic the queasy, to the delight of the drivers who love to career their vehicles near the edge for a little extra thrill.

I suspect the disciples of Jesus were not thrilled to make this steep climb, the switchback foot trails making the ascent arduous, despite the fine view. Perhaps that is why most of the apostles waited at the bottom and only the three favorites followed Jesus. They followed Jesus—that's what the journey is about. That's what Lent is about. That is what discipleship means: to follow Jesus who takes us to the strangest places, to mountaintops, into deserts, toward God's kingdom, and deep within our own souls.

There is more to the backdrop of this gospel than the fields. There is the entire Old Testament, represented by Moses and Elijah. Likewise there is always the cross. It is never far from Jesus or those who follow him. Thus, in this tranquil country place the discussion among Moses, Elijah, and Jesus centers on suffering and on Jerusalem. Those two topics always go together. There is no idle chatter here. They are not like us. These three great religious leaders talk about important matters and ultimate destinies here on the mountain. In the Bible that is what always happens on mountains. They are the places where God reveals special messages, to Moses at Sinai, to Jesus at Tabor. To us.

Jesus talked with Moses and Elijah about his passage from death to life. The Greek gospel calls this passage an "exodus," like the ancient passage of the Hebrews from slavery to freedom. Now this passage will be expanded, bringing freedom from sin and death. God's luminous glory was revealed in that ancient journey through the desert. That same glory will be revealed on this mountaintop in front of Peter, James, and John.

Jesus had gone up the mountain to pray, but the three apostles fall asleep. Later, these same three will sleep when Jesus prays in the garden of another mountain, the Mount of Olives. We disciples so easily miss the great moments! These days we would call it a "photo op" and take a picture to remember the event. Peter wanted to capture the moment by erecting tents for the main characters, but he misunderstood what was happening. Freeze-framing the moment would help no one. The only way to respond would be obeying God's command to "listen to him," to Jesus. Hearing Jesus' word is where disciples truly find God, not on mountaintops, not in deserts.

On the mountaintop Jesus received a confirmation of his mission and his identity. He is indeed God's chosen one, God's Son. If we let the word of God transform us, transfigure us, we too can catch a glimpse of our true identity—Christian.

We can also foresee our true destiny, God's kingdom.

There are many transforming moments in each of our journeys. Sometimes we are wise enough to see this. Other times we try to alter God's plan by manipulating life and decisions and lashing out at the darkness. Instead, we need to do what the gospel says these apostles did when they were confronted with all this power and mystery of God: they were silent. When the subject is the death of Jesus, perhaps that is the only proper response. Silence. So quiet that all we hear is our next breath as we make our own journey up our own mountains, confident that because of Jesus we do not make this journey to Jerusalem or to God alone.

Questions for Reflection

1. What mountains and valleys have been part of your experience of God?

2. We live in a noisy world of technological sound. We need a place, like the top of a mountain, to find calm. Where is your quiet place?

3. Peter misunderstood what was taking place in front of him. We should find some encouragement from that, that this great leader could err. How have you mistaken the message of Jesus? What have you done to grow from your mistakes?

4. The word "cross" begins to take on new meaning for the followers of Jesus. What new meaning for Lent have you been uncovering this year from your fasting, prayer, and almsgiving?

Monday of the Second Week

Daniel 9:4–10 • Psalm 79 • Luke 6:36–38

". . . for the measure you give will be the measure you get back!"

It all started at 4:30 in the morning. The phone startled me out of an already disturbed sleep. We all know that early morning phone calls are omens of trouble. This was, but in a different way. It was no emergency. No sickness. Rather, it was a friend calling from Europe to chat! Instead of enjoying his long-distance company, I immediately let him know how stupid I thought he was for not properly calculating the six-hour time difference. "Do not judge, and you will not be judged." Jesus has a way of getting even, doesn't he? My measure to him was anger. Fortunately, he measured patience back to me.

Later in the morning the devil telephone rang again. It was immediately obvious that the caller was trying to sell me something, undoubtedly something I didn't want or need. Now I can be quite good at getting rid of these callers and I cut him off asking "Are you trying to sell me something?" The answer was "No. I just want to send you a catalogue with our church appointments." Well, to me that was selling and I again berated him for wasting my time and lying. "Do not condemn, and you will not be condemned." Jesus again. I measured a lack of patience to the unwary seller. I hope that Jesus will measure more patience to me.

The rest of the day didn't go much better. In the evening, about 6:35, I had taken my little dog out and I began to wonder if this wasn't the evening that I was supposed go to the small mission church attached to my parish for a penance service for third, fourth, and fifth graders. I quickly ran inside and there the calendar told the truth. I was 10 minutes late and 5 miles away! When I tried to get the dog in the house, he refused to come. He had found leftover muffins from yesterday's Parish Fellowship in the shrubbery next to the church. He wasn't about to give up these delicacies. I had to step through the shrubbery, into a spring mud hole, grab the dog who got his muddy paws all over me, take him to the house, clean up, drive the five miles, and find the church dark and locked and the children in regular classes and the Religious Education Coordinator more than a little miffed at me.

Being clever, I managed to turn her into the victim, scolding about not waiting and not having the service properly prepared. And so on and so on. Of course, the words of the evening's Mass jumped back at me: "Be compassionate as your Father is compassionate." Again, Jesus has a way of getting right to the heart of our sin, doesn't he? I would never want the measure I used to come back to me from this incident!

As you have surmised, this was the content of that evening homily—the story of a priest who had no compassion on the day he had to preach about compassion. God works in strange ways, indeed.

The truth of the matter is that we never know what any other person is experiencing, in a day or in a lifetime. We never fully know. Some people are good actors. Everything looks all right, but it isn't. Compassion means to "feel with" someone else. Sadness. Joy. Fear. Doubt. Hurt. Success. Lent calls us to this. Jesus calls us to this.

Today I heard Jesus saying that we need to be compassionate, certainly more compassionate than I was. Hence the words, "Be compassionate as your Father is compassionate." Hence the warning: ". . . for the measure you give will be the measure you get back!"

Lord God, you teach us good lessons in unusual ways, but usually in the ordinary affairs of life. Help me, this day of Lent, to develop a sense of humor about myself. Help me, this day of Lent, to develop a sense of compassion for others. This day of Lent, grant that I may see the lives of those around me with your eyes of understanding and patience. Help me, this day of Lent, I pray! Amen.

Tuesday of the Second Week

Isaiah 1:10,16–20 • Psalm 50 • Matthew 23:1–12

"Come now, let us set things right."

Very often the heart of a Bible passage gets buried between other words that are more well known or more spectacular, or just manage to catch our attention. I think that happens with today's first reading. From the first chapter that sets the pace for the rest of Isaiah's long prophecy, words like "Sodom," "Gomorrah," "wash clean," "scarlet sin and white as snow" are familiar images. In the middle of these words we find a most important sentence that holds within it a powerful teaching about God.

"Come now, let us set things right," says the Lord! Look at them carefully. So often God's words come to us as commandments. Here we read a gentle invitation, "Come now." God is inviting us to join in accomplishing the singular activity of Lent, actually the activity that should occupy much of our lives—to set things right. We do not have to do it alone! God wants to work with us.

It is an invitation issued to all. To set things right. It doesn't take much effort to mess things up, to create problems, become a problem, to hurt, to be hurt. The healing is always more difficult than the injury, isn't it? Yet, here is our God inviting us to fix up our lives.

That's only half of the hidden power of this reading. The other half also gets lost. God says, "Let us," not just "Now you do this!" God doesn't put all the responsibility for reconciliation and repair upon our shoulders. God knows human nature too well and is too loving to do that. Nor does God simply say, "Leave it all to me. I'll fix it." Instead, God respects our human will and understands our weaknesses. God wants to work with us, mixing the human and divine, in order to bring about the "right things" that are God's promise to those who hear the word.

Our life with God is not just a series of one-way streets, God to us or us to God. The truth is that it is a partnership. The Bible calls it a covenant. "Let us work together." Those are wonderful words, an invitation to action, a statement of understanding, a reflection of God's love and respect for us.

Jesus shows that he understands these words of Isaiah quoted in the gospel. Whenever we become too absorbed with our own roles, as Pharisee, as scribe, as religious leaders, as teachers, as parents, we need to hear this gospel passage that calls us to a right relationship with others. It is so easy to let the relationships become lopsided: in a classroom, in a family, in a marriage, in a parish. In the Christian community, signed and sealed in baptism, that relationship, that "setting things right," can mean only one thing: imitating the example of Jesus to serve others with all our talents and energy and love.

That is an effort worthy of our Lent. How will you respond to God's invitation? "Come now, let us set things right!"

Lord God, so often I lose a sense of my partnership with you. I want you to do it all, or I feel I should do it all. Even though I celebrate the mystery of your covenant with us at each Mass, I lose sight of your real desire to have me work with you in re-creating myself this Lent and in re-creating our world in your image. May I learn to heed the summons you issued through Isaiah long ago: "Come, now, let us set things right." Help me to make myself right in your eyes and in your love. Amen.

Wednesday of the Second Week

Jeremiah 18:18–20 • Psalm 31 • Matthew 20:17–28

"What is it you want?"

I wonder what Sigmund Freud would have thought about our two readings and psalm in today's liturgy. The founder of modern psychology, he has had an influence on our lives and has made many ideas and terms popular. One of those is "paranoia," the unfounded idea that someone is out to get us. I cannot help but imagine he would have a field day examining the ideas found in today's readings. Each of them confronts that inner terror which can also be the stalking and controlling reality of life. Is something or someone out to get us? Or, in the words of the gospel, "What is it that we really want?" Out of life? From one another? From God?

Jeremiah had reason to fear. All he wanted was to be left alone, but it was not to be. Once he accepted God's will for him rather than his own, he turned prophet, a powerful spokesman for God and for God's truth. His words of truth had disturbed the population of Jerusalem so deeply that the people were angry and the leaders wanted to drive him from the city. In fact, they wanted to kill him. They considered his teaching a heresy; his deeds were traitorous.

The psalmist offers a similar scenario. Hushed whispers frighten him. Plotting adversaries seek to overcome him. Intrigue and danger are the backdrop for his words. What he wanted from God was physical safety and spiritual assurance.

In the gospel, Jesus too knows that there is a price for God's truth. It has always been so. Sadly enough, the price is often death. As Jesus and the disciples turn toward Jerusalem, an uphill journey both geographically and spiritually, he knows that his words of truth will meet harsh opposition, an opposition that will be satisfied only with his death.

This is no unreasonable sense of opposition. It is not paranoia. Not for Jesus or for Jeremiah or for the psalmist. Though whispered, the threats are real. Jesus and Jeremiah shared many common traits. They spoke God's truth, lived God's law, offered God's love. How odd that anyone would be threatened because of this, but people always have been threatened by what they perceive as contrary to their own interests. The real paranoia lies not with Jesus or Jeremiah, but with those others who found that God's way was too much for them. What they wanted was an easy religion, a cheap salvation.

In our own time, too, religion finds itself in trouble. Religious belief and secular influences battle for our loyalty. Even when we do all we can in the name of God's love, not everyone understands, appreciates it, or accepts it. It doesn't put cash in the register.

Those who battle against God's initiatives are the frightened ones. Those who struggle with what God is trying to do in their lives understand the tension, but like Jeremiah and Jesus and the psalmist, they place their trust in God's love and power, which is ever active, not against us but for us.

Jesus ends the gospel passage with a reminder of his mission: to give an example of service. There will always be those who prefer to *be* served. When the price of the service is free, like the multiplied bread at the lakeside, or when the master washes the feet of his servants, the world becomes confused. Confusion leads to suspicion. In turn, suspicion leads to a reaction of self-preservation. The world cannot understand that salvation, though free, was not cheap.

A real disciple of Jesus comes to understand this. The question of Jesus, "What do you want?" is answered differently then. No seeking for self. No search for power. The follower of Jesus knows this and accepts it. The follower of Jesus doesn't let the anxiety of the world undo the simple, necessary lesson of the gospel: serve the rest. That is what God has done since creation. That is what Jesus did in his ministry. That is what Lent calls us to do.

Lord God, somehow it is reassuring to know that others feel as I do, that others sense frustration at trying so hard to do what is right and just. For the prophets and for Jesus, it was on a grander scale than my life, but in my own life I need the reassurance that comes from knowing that others feel as I do. I am no prophet like Jeremiah, but grant that I may speak your truth. I am no savior like Jesus, but help me to bring his love into my life and into my world. Amen.

Thursday of the Second Week

Jeremiah 17:5–10 • Psalm 1 • Luke 16:19–31

Blessed are those who trust in the Lord.

We live in a strange time. Perhaps any time in history is strange, but we know our own times best and they are odd. To many, the approach of a new century is a welcome arrival. It means the end of a century that has witnessed the worst devastation of human beings that we have inflicted on one another. Human beings have caused these disasters and we look to other human beings to solve the problems. History shows that this is often a disastrous course. Trust in God is what is needed, but this is usually missing.

That was true in the time of Jeremiah when people trusted in armies to save them. Instead, the national army failed and a foreign army conquered. Trusting in God seemed too frail and uncertain. Too distant.

What makes this time in history peculiar in our part of the world is the gradual erosion of spirituality. We have all grown up hearing words about the division of "body and soul" and "material and spiritual." As our part of the world has grown in power, prestige, and comfort, we all find ourselves accepting certain elements of our culture as normal and even good. For example, there are few homes without at least one television set. VCRs abound. Even if we are on the "poorer" side of the tracks, we have so much compared to other people in the world. Anyone who has ever traveled to a third world nation knows this. Our children grow up expecting material things and opportunities. Our culture tells us that all this is good and that money makes the good life possible.

Lost, somewhere, is a sense of spirituality. This is not the totally "other worldly" spirituality of the Middle Ages. It is simply a sense of who we really are: body *and* soul. This is the part of us that our culture intends to ignore because it cannot be bought, sold, measured, or moved from place to place. Now during Lent we always expect to think about these things with greater seriousness, and today's readings force us to look squarely at our lives, at our spirituality, at our true selves.

Jeremiah's plaintive prophecy demands that we look beyond the measured material parts of our lives. There is more to our existence than our possessions that we insure and lock up against loss or theft. Our hope should be in God, not in handbags, bank accounts, securities, and property. True, such things all play a part in our lives, but we easily tend to make them the whole of our lives.

The gospel brings the same message to us even more forcibly. Although it is a parable, it packs the punch of reality. Since our own comfort is often bought and paid for by other people's suffering, it is so easy to turn a deaf ear to the many pleas for help that come to us. The poor, the unfortunate, the downtrodden, the underdogs of this world know that even though there are many good people in the world, there are not enough. There are far too many cheats, greedy people, and "users." Hence, Jeremiah's advice to "trust in the Lord." That is exactly what the beggar of the parable had to do. He could not trust in people, certainly not in the rich man. The poor Lazarus who begged for food teaches a blunt lesson: In the kingdom of God, things will be reversed. Those who were ignored will enjoy God's company. We who eat and drink in comfort will lose out on the joys of God's kingdom.

In the end, our final judgment is of our own making. Our attitude and response to our neighbor's needs, here and now, will be the witness before God. All the smooth words and wishful intentions of our lives will be too late then.

If we really trust in the Lord, we are willing to give up, to do without, to sacrifice. When we trust only in ourselves, in our treasures and our wiles, we reveal that we really don't trust in the Lord, no matter how fine our words of prayer might be. Both Jeremiah and the gospel are clear: our actions reveal just how much we truly "trust in the Lord." Once again, the "performance principle" of the gospel looks us straight in the eye and quotes to us the final words of Jeremiah's prophecy from today's reading: "I the Lord alone probe the mind and test the heart, to reward everyone according to his ways, according to the merit of his deeds." If we really trust in the Lord, we would be willing to give up, to do without, to sacrifice, to give alms, to make Lent work.

Lord God, almsgiving—even the word sounds antiquated, but it is so real. So necessary. Let the message of this gospel sink deeply into my soul. Let its challenge open my eyes to the needs of the bigger world around me. Let me trust you more and more to help me, to help us all. Although prayer helps, so do the material things that others need. Make me generous and help me to give cheerfully. Help me to make this an important part of my Lent. Amen.

Friday of the Second Week

Genesis 37:3–4,12–13,17–28 • Psalm 105
Matthew 21:33–43,45–46

"He is our brother, our own flesh!"

Human nature changes very little over the decades, or even over the millennia. We see that clearly in these familiar lenten readings. Joseph's brothers are envious of him because his father, Jacob, shows favoritism for him, one of many sons. This alone augurs trouble. Joseph is either fool enough or confident enough to tell his older brothers about his dreams in which they end up showing deference to a younger brother. In the world they lived in, this just isn't done!

Their concern was not just the long tunic that Jacob gave Joseph. That was envy. There was also their greed, for the coat represented favoritism and perhaps their father would bestow the entire inheritance upon this favored, younger son. With greed and envy destroying their souls, they took action against their father and brother. "He is our brother, our own flesh!" but that has seldom stopped people from acting on their selfishness.

Families seem to have a hard time of it in the Bible. Cain killed his brother Abel. Now, once again, brothers plot a murder. Only the intercession of two brothers blocks the evil deed. Instead, they sell him to foreigners on their way to Egypt. In their minds, Joseph is as good as dead, gone. Their plotting worked. A pesky younger brother is done away with, but without the danger of blood guilt on their hands. The risk to their own inheritance is gone and they can continue to court their father's favor. So much for true family loyalty!

The gospel tells a similar tale. Jesus must have been in a feisty mood that day; he surely knew that his parable would provoke, not entertain, his lofty audience.

The chief priests and elders knew well that the image of the vineyard came from Isaiah (5:1–7), who had used this image to describe the way God carefully cultivated a favored vine, his people Israel. Instead of yielding plump, tasty grapes, though, the vine brought forth sour grapes and thistles. Isaiah's prophecy was a scolding for the people of Israel; Jesus' parable was a scolding for the people of his own day. In neither case did the people react favorably.

Once again the favored son, heir to the entire estate, is mal-treated by the very people whom the wealthy owner cared for. This son wasn't the flesh brother of the people who leased the vineyard, but in the eyes of God all people are brothers and sisters, all deserving respect, regardless of the biological rela-tionship. Human nature—people—doesn't easily learn to change, to harken to God's constant plea to take care of itself, to correct itself.

The early church repeated the parable, knowing well what had happened to Jesus. The parable helped those first believ-ers to justify their mission to the Gentiles, to anyone who would pay attention to God and to God's son. Those who should have paid attention did not.

Both Joseph and Jesus were the victims of other people's greed and envy. Lent reminds us that we are always faced with the choice to join the crowds who push Jesus aside in order to continue with the pursuit of personal gain and ful-fillment, or to choose to take Jesus most seriously and to give of our time, talent, and treasure in pursuit of God's kingdom.

God began this good work in us, planting the seed of faith. Our forty days of Lent give us time to cultivate the seed and to grow in our own understanding of faith so we will be among those who yield a rich harvest. The lenten practice of prayer should help to correct our envy because prayer helps us to keep a healthy balance between genuine need and the desire for more. Almsgiving should correct our greed, because instead of wanting more and more for ourselves we donate money and goods to help others. Envy and greed: two capital sins. This Lent, we struggle to identify how they tempt us to deny Jesus, but with these readings in hand, we can overcome them.

"He is our brother, our own flesh." Lent asks us to recognize this reality in one another, to see the relationships we share because God has created us all in the divine image and likeness.

Lord God, sometimes I'm the rejected one. Sometimes I'm the one who rejects others, who scoffs and scorns them. Sometimes I feel sorry for Joseph and think I'm just like him. Other times, I'm the envious sibling. Grant that I may put aside pettiness and jealousy and see the simple truth that you choose all people, that you care for all people, that all people are welcome in your kingdom. Amen.

Saturday of the Second Week

Micah 7:14–15,18–20 • Psalm 103 • Luke 15:1–3,11–32

"He was lost and is found."

Every school, every parish, in fact, just about every public place has a lost and found department. A whole room or a box on a table, it's where misplaced or forgotten items end up. No matter how they got lost, no matter what the item is, precious or junk, it ends up there. Sometimes it seems that there should be a "lost and found" for people too, a place where we can go when we begin to lose our way to God or to one another or to our own souls.

That's what this gospel is about, this most familiar of all parables, about a younger son who loses his way through life. It is also about an older son who loses his way in the world. It is about all of us who at one time or another get lost in this confusing, hurtful world and need to get found again. Who need to find our way again.

We are eventually found! That's the good news, and the good news gets even better because Jesus insists in this parable that it is no one less than God who finds us as we wander around, wondering about life.

When we were in school, teachers would often give "fill-in-the-blank" tests. We had to write in just the right word to show that we understood the subject. We should do the same thing some time in our churches to see what everyone's image of God is: God is _____. The answers would depend on people's experience of life, of God, and of other people. Some might say "God is omnipotent." Or "God is all-knowing." Other words in the blank might be "powerful," "creator," "judge." The list could go on and on.

Our readings today suggest a different insight into God.

The anonymous psalmist tells us that "God is kind and merciful." I wonder how many people would list those as the *first* adjectives for God. Jesus tells us that God is the lost and found department of the world!

Both the prophet Micah and Jesus thought the same response would be appropriate. Look again at Micah: "Who is like you, the God who removes guilt and pardons sin for the remnant of his inheritance; who does not persist in anger forever but delights rather in clemency, and will again have compassion on us?"

What an image of God! The almighty, all-knowing God, the creator of the universe and the judge of heaven and earth, is, in fact, always stooping toward this planet of ours, toward us, in order to dispense not judgment and punishment, but forgiveness and mercy! Micah's words are filled with this wonderful, gentle image of God! In Lent, when we focus so much of our attention on our failings, it is a great comfort to know that God is more concerned with healing and helping than with vindication.

Jesus must have read Micah often, for the parable of the "prodigal son" contains a description of Micah's God in terms that the Palestinian population of his day would find most unusual. Fathers were usually harsh, in control, in every way master of what they owned. The typical man of that society was much concerned about "saving face" and being respected in the small community he lived in, where everybody knew everybody else's business!

This remarkable father in the parable doesn't care about the stereotype of how he ought to behave toward his wayward son. His love for his sons gushes out of him, first for the younger son who had run away and then for the envious older son whose harsh words were cutting and cruel.

Jesus tells us that God is like that father. There isn't the slightest hint of punishment or even rebuke in the father, is there? There is only goodness, forgiveness, acceptance of each son as he is. That's the way God accepts us! That's the way God finds us, and it's always OK.

It's easy to get lost in our world or even in our own little worlds. Lent gives us time to stand still for a few moments and to let God "find" us. It also gives us time to think about our own compassion, the need to forgive, and to accept ourselves and others.

God is kind and merciful and will find us, all of us, sooner or later. And then this same God takes us home again, no longer lost souls, but people who find that God is the way.

Lord God, let me experience your kindness and mercy. Help me to know those qualities by exercising them in my dealings with others. Kindness and mercy, that is the lesson of your prophets and of Jesus. When I feel lost in myself, let me remember this gospel. When I feel I'm just wandering through life, let me remember the overflowing love of your forgiveness and your relentless search to find me. Most of all, let me celebrate that "I was lost and now am found." May this Saturday of Lent, so filled with things to do, be filled with kindness and mercy. Amen.

THIRD WEEK OF LENT

Lent is beginning to wear on most people by now. The practices of fasting, dutiful prayer, and almsgiving are revealing more and more of who we really are. Have we been strong enough to be faithful to our Ash Wednesday intentions? Do we notice changes taking place within us? Around us? Because of us?

This third week of Lent begins to urge us to journey more deeply into the movement of Lent. Our pilgrimage should be taking us closer and closer to God, so it is no surprise that this Sunday, and throughout this third week, we are brought face to face with gospels that challenge and puzzle us, almost as though God is giving a little shove to keep us on the move.

Just in case that hasn't been happening, the readings this week almost attack us with a consistent bluntness. Religion is serious business, not frosting on the cake. Lent is serious business, and the more seriously we take it, the more we benefit from it.

We meet an interesting cast of characters this week, in the Sunday readings as well as the daily revelations. We meet famous believers (Moses, Jeremiah, Hosea) and even more famous unbelievers. Sometimes those who do not believe take refuge in anonymity. That's the easy way out, to hide in the crowd. But Lent doesn't let us melt away into the crowd too easily. Believe. Reform. Forgive. Those are the key words to this third week.

To make this week of Lent a little more beneficial, you might consider:

1. Prayer: Go to a local Catholic bookstore and pick up a good Way of the Cross or other booklet to help you pray.

2. Fasting: Keep track of what you've done to fast, not just the calories and pounds, but the dollars too. Perhaps you might contribute the money you've saved to some special cause.

3. Almsgiving: Start some spring cleaning and give away items that you really don't need any longer. At Thanksgiving and Christmas, local food pantries often get overstocked because the season brings out our kindness. The need is great at this time of the year too. You might make your own contribution or gather food from neighbors as well.

Third Sunday of Lent
Year A

Exodus 17:3–7 • Romans 5:1–2,5–8 • John 4:5–42

A grumbling crowd. An anonymous woman. A confrontation. Jesus. We do well to place ourselves in these situations, to costume ourselves as one of the characters and then see if the truth of the story begins to take shape inside us.

All our stories begin with sin. That's where God usually finds us, in some hurtful place in our lives. Lost in a desert or alone at the well. That's where our Bible begins—in sin. It ends in salvation, which is where all the stories ultimately lead. God has promised us that happy ending.

Exodus reminds us that the journey in between is difficult. From slavery in Egypt to salvation in the desert: that's quite a journey. The people never let Moses forget it. They complained, they grumbled, they even preferred slavery in Egypt to this desert's freedom where they thirsted.

Certainty is always easier than risk. Their physical thirst was real but it was only a shadow of the spiritual thirst that was the true problem. The passage from slavery to freedom, from unbelief to belief, is difficult. It was for the Hebrews and it is for us. We all complain along life's way. God listens to a lot of complaining! What matters, though, is that God listens!

This wonderful gospel teaches a similar lesson! The woman at the well is each of us, struggling with life, questioning God's will and wisdom, then finally making an act of faith. We too meet Jesus, often in these ordinary activities of life. We talk with him, struggle with his gospel and with his cross, and then come to him as Savior.

The woman and Jesus ask each other questions. We all have to answer them. Who are you? What do you need? What gets in your way of answering the first two questions? First, who are you? The woman sees Jesus, a Jew, an enemy. Then she begins to grow in understanding. She recognizes that he is a prophet. Finally she comes to understand that this man is the messiah. The God she meets at the well is tired and in need, a bit of a nuisance. He is in her way. Later she will discover that he is the way.

Jesus sees a woman, a clever and attractive woman—five times married! Some say that is why she comes to the well at noon, because the other women of the village would shun her. They knew what she was: a sinner. Others say that she comes at noon because then the sun is brightest, the light of the world and the light of the sun coming together for a wonderful revelation.

In either case, the gospel makes us answer the questions. Who are you? Be honest. Lent forces us to answer. What do others see in you? A tired image and likeness of God? A sinner, evading truthful answers? A seeker, dialoguing with Jesus? Who are you?

Second, what do you need? We know what we want, but few of us know what we need. Jesus needed water and rest. The woman thought that she needed only water. What she really needed was Jesus. Some understanding. Acceptance. Faith. Jesus gave her these gifts by talking with her, by caring for her. He did it by sharing his faith with her, not some textbook answer, but his own experience of God. But enough of Jesus and the woman. What do you need?

Third, what gets in the way? For Jesus, nothing. He broke down the barriers. He always does that. Never mind that she was a Samaritan. Never mind that rabbis shouldn't talk to strange women. Jesus never let bad rules get in the way. The woman, like all of us, had a story and attitudes that got in the way. Even this strange man at the well was an obstacle at first.

There is so much that blocks our way to God. It is easier just to complain, but Lent demands that we clear away the clutter that complicates our lives. We're all somewhere in this story, aren't we? We're all somewhere on the road between sin and salvation, between being sinners and being saved.

The woman at the well was lucky. She met the stranger who shared his God. The woman came to faith because she took time to talk with Jesus. It takes time. It takes sharing. God loves us enough to give us both. God loves us enough to give us Lent. God loves us enough to give us Jesus.

Questions for Reflection

1. Why is it that Catholics are not as willing to talk about their religion as other people? Why are we "shy" about our religion?

2. Complaints are often honest expressions of need, fear, and frustration. What prayer or complaints do you offer to God? How is God responding to you?

3. What gets in your way of being the (religious) person you want to be?

Third Sunday of Lent
Year B

Exodus 20:1–17 • 1 Corinthians 1:22–25 • John 2:13–25

"You are my people. I am your God." These two sentences sum up the heart of biblical faith. These words are the absolute affirmation of God's attitude toward us, the people of God. Again in Lent we enter into the life of ancient Israel. Dramatic events and unparalleled love bring us to the mountain of God, Horeb. In the wasteland of the wilderness, God gathers people. The power of the storm abates; the blowing of the shofar ceases. All is quiet. The whole world holds its breath to hear what God will speak to Moses. To the Hebrews. To us. God will speak, but what will God say? How will Israel listen? How will we listen?

God speaks: "I am the Lord your God who brought you out of the land of Egypt, that house of bondage." That is what God does for us, sets us free. In return, God asks fidelity, to be faithful to a way of life that will continue to set us free from our bondage to selfishness and sin.

The Hebrew people came to know God better by following God in the desert for forty years. There God revealed provident care, endless compassion, power for the sake of others, and faithful companionship. God also made it clear that we must learn to respect God and live in peace with one another. To assure this, God gave us commandments. Ten of them are well known. We read them in today's first reading. They are what God asks of us while continuing to care for us and lavish protection and gifts upon us.

Make no mistake. They are commandments. "Do not kill! Do not steal! " They reflect a simplicity and directness that is uncomplicated by detail or the trivial. These commandments are the heart of a covenant, the agreement that God writes into the stone tablets. "You are my people. I am your God." This covenant, this solemn pact, is the same agreement we enter at our baptism. At each Eucharist we renew it and renew our union with God in Christ through the blood of the new covenant. Slowly, through each year's Lent, we move toward Easter and the renewal of our baptismal covenant.

Jesus knew how these commandments reach into the heart, and he applied them to his own life. He also knew how we try to weasel around them, looking for ways to make God's law more convenient.

The Old Testament is very clear about these commandments. If you follow them, you live; if you ignore them, the result is death. The ancient tribal society that first heard these words knew well that every clan member had to follow these laws. As a result, each person knew what to expect from the other. Fidelity from each member assured peace in the community, the harmony the Bible calls *shalom*.

To break the commandments and to violate the agreement we share and renew in the Eucharist—that is sin. Such sin fractures the fragile relationships that sustain our lives. Implicit in our baptismal covenant is the acknowledgment that each person is loved by God and redeemed by Christ, that each is a brother or sister worthy of affection and concern and respect. By faithful adherence to the covenant, to God's law, especially the law of love, we strengthen our union with God and with others.

To believe that genuine care for each person is the only proper way to live seems foolish and weak to the world, but at baptism we chose this fundamental value—to live for Christ and others. During Lent we expend our energies to strengthen the covenant bonds that may be weakened during the year. During Lent we work at fixing up the damage we have done to ourselves and others. We cleanse ourselves of the attitudes and actions that impair or even sever our relationships to God and others.

"I am your God. You are my people." We are in this pilgrimage to the kingdom of God together. What does God ask of us this Lent?

Questions for Reflection

1. Our baptismal covenant binds us together. What are some ways that your way of life reflects this union?

2. Who are the persons in your life that you need to seek out this Lent in order to repair the past damages of sin?

3. What prejudices and discrimination are present in your life because of race, language, creed, or history?

4. If you could accomplish any single goal this Lent, what would it be? How can you make this happen?

Third Sunday of Lent
Year C

Exodus 3:1–8,13–15 • 1 Corinthians 10:1–6,10–12
Luke 13:1–9

Many years ago I served at a large urban parish where a great weeping willow graced the rectory's front lawn. It provided shade and beauty. Late one summer it was obvious that the tree was not doing well. It would have to be cut down. I lamented about this to an elderly gentleman in the parish whose backyard garden was a local miracle. He could grow cabbage the size of bowling balls. If anyone had a green thumb, he did. His suggestion for the tree: drill holes in the ground around the periphery of the branches, one every 18 inches, and pour in fertilizer. Within a week the "sick" tree showed signs of new vitality. The temptation was to eliminate the problem quickly with an axe. What was needed was time, competence, and caring.

The gospel for this third Sunday of Lent was the occasion for remembering that long past moment. It is a strange gospel with an unusual assortment of events. It's difficult to determine why we read it during Lent; however, a more careful second reading uncovers some interesting lessons.

It begins like an ancient news broadcast: Galileans (whose tendencies to revolt against Rome were notorious) are killed at the order of Pilate, who was notorious in his own right. Perhaps they were executed while offering sacrifice in the Temple! Jesus does not condemn Pilate. Ironically, it is Pilate who will later condemn Jesus. Nor does Jesus offer any opinion about the cause of the Galilean revolutionaries. In the face of this evil, Jesus remains neutral, but he reminds his listeners—that is always us—that we should worry more about our own repentance and our own relationship with God and neighbor.

The next "news byte" recalls the accidental collapse of a tower that killed eighteen people. Great, sudden tragedy happens all the time and we all wonder why, but Jesus sees things differently. When asked if the victims of this natural disaster were being punished for something they did, he focuses on what really matters: that we genuinely change our lives and not worry about events beyond our control; we should fix our own lives, which we can control. Twice Jesus advises us: "Unless you begin to reform, you will all come to the same end."

Those words are the key to this gospel—and to Lent. This weekend brings us to the middle of Lent, but have we yet begun to take it seriously? Have we begun to reform? Or are we still much the same, to our own disappointment?

The parable of the fig tree says it all. "There's still time." It's so easy to tell ouselves that we'll begin tomorrow! The fig tree should produce fruit ten months a year, yet whenever the owner went out to check on it, there wasn't any. It was a drain on the meagre water resources of the land. Like the willow tree in front of the rectory, it was in danger of being cut down. Sometimes we feel we are the fig tree and that God will cut us down, but perhaps we are the ones who cut God out of our lives when our hopes seem to falter or when our plans to change fail or our dreams collapse, like towers in the rain.

Then remember the parable: God gives us time to change. A lifetime. Jesus is always there, intereceding for us with God and helping us because none of us alone has all the resources we need to grow in faith and make all the changes we want to make. We need Jesus for that. We need Lent for that. We need one another, too.

The parable doesn't say whether the owner granted the reprieve or whether the tree produced any fruit. I drove past that rectory recently to see if the tree was still there. It was, healthy and beautiful as ever. Time, competence, and caring were all it needed. That's what we need too. Only we can write the final line of the parable. What conclusion are you writing with this year's Lent?

Questions for Reflection

1. What "second chance" do you need to give yourself this Lent?

2. Who in your circle of relations needs a second chance from you?

3. What recent "disaster," either personal or natural, has left you puzzled about God's will?

4. Is there someone you have cut out of your life recently? Why? Can you make amends this Lent?

5. How is your prayer, fasting, and almsgiving going so far?

Monday of the Third Week

2 Kings 5:1–15 • Psalm 42 • Luke 4:24–30

"No prophet gains acceptance in his native place."

Not long ago I led a pilgrimage of parishioners to the Holy Land. While we visited the holy sites of Galilee, we stayed in Nazareth, the town of today's gospel. I had asked for accommodations at a hotel that was familiar to me, centrally located and famous for its simple but good food. Upon arrival I learned that other arrangements had been made for us, I suspect to the profit of the tour company.

The place was beautiful in its own right, but it was distant from the center of Nazareth. There were no nearby restaurants or sites. The winter chill of the Galilean hills pervaded the place, especially when the electricity went off, which was often! I tried to calm the rising anger of the tour group by explaining that "pilgrimages are supposed to have their share of discomfort and inconvenience."

That explanation was acceptable for the moment, but I was beginning to feel that "I wasn't accepted" and had better not push my luck! But then, this gospel came to mind. There we were, on the brow of the hill upon which Nazareth had been built, the same brow of the hill that the folks of biblical times wanted to use as the instrument of Jesus' death!

Our tour group was congenial, but nonetheless irked by the cold and inconvenience. What was it, so long ago, that had irked the good people of Nazareth to want to kill their famous son? Jesus had just finished a wonderful sermon, the gospel tells us, and everyone was singing his praises. But as always, there were others whose envy was stirred, who remembered his humble origins and weren't about to have him lecture them! That's always part of human life, isn't it? The better our friends and acquaintances think they know us, the less, often, they really know us. Jesus couldn't be accepted in his native place because people thought they knew who he was, the neighbor kid.

They turned on Jesus, and he, in turn, used his best weapon against them: the truth. In Old Testament times a terrible drought and famine had swept over this part of the country. The lack of water was real enough, but as often happens in the Bible, it meant much more than "no rain"; it symbolized the lack of faith, the spiritual dryness of the people.

Jesus reminds the townspeople of two events in their own history. One was that great drought; the other was a famous cure. During the drought and subsequent famine the great Elijah invoked God's loving power to feed a starving foreigner! Israel's lack of faith was its own hunger for God. In the other episode, there were many lepers in the land, but Elisha the prophet healed a foreigner's leprosy. In turn, Namaan the Syrian came to believe in the power of God, whereas the local people played games with God.

These stern reminders irritated the folks of Nazareth. Recalling that Elijah left his native place to prophesy elsewhere and that Elisha preached to his own, who didn't listen, the Nazareth villagers knew well that Jesus was not just teaching a history lesson but was pointing the experience directly at them: You are like your ancestors! You don't accept those sent to you. You don't truly believe, and so neither God nor I can help you.

Outwardly, all was well. The people were praying in the synagogue. All looked good. But it wasn't. Inside they were unhealthy; their souls were far from God.

We are nearing the middle of Lent. If we've taken Lent seriously, there might be family members or acquaintances who are finding us just a little different these days. Perhaps they are not open to the changed persons we are or accept how serious we have become about spirituality and faith. Our fasting may be showing some signs of tangible results. Our alms-giving may be reducing the amount of our ready cash. Our prayer time may be greater.

This gospel calls us to look inside ourselves as well, our motivations and honest thoughts about Lent, Jesus, ourselves, and others. We need to be sure that Jesus is not just passing by our lives, but that we are continuing the truly hard work of Lent: listening to Jesus' truthful words, letting them get inside of us and change us, and continuing to walk toward our Easter rendezvous with Jesus.

Lord God, my own pilgrimage through Lent is a mirror of my pilgrimage through life. Sometimes I like to listen to your Son; other times I find his words too demanding, too hard to bear. Be with me today as I begin another week of hearing and living your powerful, truthful word. Let my own words be true and compassionate. Jesus' relatives and neighbors turned on him. Help me not to turn on those closest to me, but to see them as the first who deserve my caring hand and prayer. Amen.

Tuesday of the Third Week

Daniel 3:25,34–43 • Psalm 25 • Matthew 18:21–35

"Should you not have dealt mercifully . . . as I did with you?"

"Forgive us our trespasses as we forgive those who trespass against us." How often we pray those words! They are among the first words we learn to pray as children. We pray them at every Mass and they are prayed over us when we die. Just two weeks ago today we heard these famous words in the gospel. In a slightly different way we hear them again today.

I suspect that Jesus' teaching about forgiveness had caught people off-guard. We have grown up learning about forgiveness, how important it is, how generous God's forgiveness is and how our own forgiveness should be equally generous. Yet, for the people who listened to Jesus, his insistence on the *absolute* generous forgiveness of the all-powerful God was startling. The Old Testament reading from Daniel and the gospel today insist on the quality of mercy. It's not that people didn't hope in and believe in God's forgiveness; life would be unbearable without it. But the breadth of God's mercy and the insistence that we treat others the same—not just once a year on the Day of Atonement, but all the time—this was something new. The idea that God would deal mercifully with us in the measure that we are merciful, that was something to ponder!

Jesus' followers had to be puzzled at this. I can see them talking about it among themselves, when Jesus wasn't around, or musing over it while walking silently from village to village. How they must have marveled at the things Jesus said and did!

Today, in this reading, Peter thinks he has figured it out! Perhaps he has been quarreling with his brother Andrew. Brothers in the Bible are known to do that. Just ask Cain and

Abel, or Joseph and his brothers. Or perhaps Peter is just speaking figuratively. At any rate, he approaches Jesus with the bold suggestion that offering forgiveness seven times is a rather generous gesture! He was probably quite pleased that he had come to this conclusion. But it was a calculated, measured forgiveness, wasn't it? It was not the generous, overflowing abundant mercy that comes, without thinking, from the heart.

Then, with great patience, Jesus explains his teaching and goes even further. Seven times is nothing. Seventy times seven—that's more like it! Limitless forgiveness is the only acceptable measure. Calculated forgiveness is no forgiveness.

God forgives everyone and everything. God's compassion surpasses anything our experience can conjure. That is the teaching of Jesus. Then comes this parable, a story to bring out the meaning of the Our Father's words on forgiveness.

"Forgive us as we forgive others!" The miserable servant did not imitate his master's goodness. Right there are the teeth of the lesson: God is like the master, forgiving all. All too often we are like the servant: petty and stingy with our forgiveness. Whenever we feel that happening to us, we need to remember this lenten lesson. "My heavenly Father will treat you in exactly the same way unless you forgive one another from your hearts." Forgiveness for all, from the heart: there's a goal worthy of our Lent.

Lord God, Jesus teaches me what forgiveness is. How that lesson should be shouted from the housetops! Your compassion for us is boundless. This Lent, help me to recall the times I needed forgiveness from others and received it. Help me also to review all my relationships that are strained and give me the courage to take the right steps to repair the damage I have done, to forgive and be reconciled. I ask this grace through Christ our Lord. Amen.

Wednesday of the Third Week

Deuteronomy 4:1,5–9 • Psalm 147 • Matthew 5:17–19

"Whoever fulfills and teaches these commands shall be great in the kingdom of God."

My desk is home to many Bibles, several English translations as well as several copies of Greek and Hebrew originals. As luck (or Providence) had it, today I had the Hebrew Bible open to Deuteronomy while preparing this reflection. One of the parish workers stopped by and saw this unusual writing in the book and asked about it. "Perfect!" I thought. Here was the chance to give an example of today's lesson.

I showed him the beautiful letters on the page, and explained how in Hebrew a tiny dash (called a tittle) can make the difference between a letter being an "R" or a "B" or a "K" or a "P" in Hebrew. By way of example, if you wrote the letters "at," which letter do you put in front of it: r, for rat? b, for bat? p, for pat? Or c, for a cat? So, in Hebrew, a tiny dash, almost invisible, makes all the difference in the meaning!

How much more important that difference is when the word of God is the subject we are dealing with! To this day Jewish people love to debate the meaning of their ancient law: what the commandments mean, how to observe them in different times, and so on. They enjoy arguing over which commandments are more important and why. There were the "heavy commandments" and the "light commandments." Every one of them helps people to live according to God's will and in harmony with their neighbor. Jesus certainly was involved in that activity. "Whoever fulfills and teaches these commandments shall be great in the kingdom of God." Jesus was such a teacher. But more than just teaching, he also observed all the commandments.

Sadly, in our own time we know how quickly some people accuse others of false teaching. This gospel shows that Jesus had enemies too, people who seriously disagreed with his interpretation of the ancient Jewish law (the Torah) or the teachings of the prophets. His defense is quick: he is not changing any of the letters of the law, not adding a tiny dash or eliminating one. Rather, he is teaching the true meaning of religious law.

This passage from Deuteronomy gives us a glimpse into the spirit of that law. It is not a burden. Quite the contrary, it is a delight. Where there is law, we know what to do. There is no guesswork. Wise people follow laws because the result is, generally, peace and harmony. Little is left to chance.

Jesus understood that spirit of Deuteronomy. Teaching the way to God was not a matter of looking for shortcuts or doing the least necessary. Lazy students like to slip by with those kinds of efforts. The concern here is nothing less than life with God. Everything possible ought to be done. Instead of looking for the easy way out, Lent calls us to do more than usual, to direct our energies toward active almsgiving and works of kindness and to direct our souls deeper and deeper into the full meaning of God's word. "Whoever fulfills and teaches these commands shall be great in the kingdom of God."

Lord God, sometimes your laws seem to be too much, demanding and harsh. It is often difficult to see how law can direct my heart to you and to my neighbor. Some people want more laws; others want less. Grant that I may not worry so much about such things, but instead do all that I can to grow in grace during this season. Plant your law in my heart. Let your Son be my guide in your ways. Amen.

Thursday of the Third Week

Jeremiah 7:23–28 • Psalm 95 • Luke 11:14–23

"It is by Beelzebul that he casts out devils."

God has a sense of humor. There is no doubt about it. How else do we explain some of the strange coincidences that befall us in a lifetime? Or is what we consider coincidence actually part of God's plan? For some, it may come with the timing of things. With others, it is the juxtaposition of events that seems providential. I often find that just when I have said or done something I thought marvelously right or incredibly stupid or shameful, the next day's readings point it out to me and confirm either my faith or my frailty.

In this gospel, Jesus' enemies claim it is by Beelzebul that Jesus casts out devils, using that name as a title for the devil. Actually, the term means "lord of the flies," an apt title for God's adversary, especially in the hot world of the Middle East. The word itself is a corruption of the name of a god that was worshipped long ago in that part of the world. Today one can drive from Jerusalem, toward the Mediterranean, and come to the ruins of Ekron, the biblical city that worshipped this god. His name was certainly not "lord of the flies," but by playing around with the name a bit, the Hebrews could derisively call this god by such an abominable, derogatory title. In fact, the original name was probably "lord of the habitation" or "lord of the princes."

At any rate, once again God showed me today the sense of humor that lurks behind the universe. The little mission church that I serve is in the middle of our rich farm country. Often in summer, after the church has been closed up a few days, flies find their way into its crevices and invade the old building. Every time I enter, I have to spend a few minutes vacuuming the dead flies off the floor and windowsills. I had hoped to make them a part of my homily for this day at the mission church, but since it is still winter, they were not to be found.

The point that Jesus wanted to make, of course, is that our own hearts can often be torn between loyalties—"Whoever is not with me is against me . . ." Sometimes difficult decisions involve choices between two apparent goods: what project to promote over another, what person to help before we help another, where to spend a limited amount of money or time, and so on. Our souls can be torn, too, when we are severely tempted to do what is immoral or when God's sense of humor or God's will challenges us.

Today's gospel reminds us that Lent gives us time to strengthen ourselves for these tensions, for the influences that compete for our loyalties. Beelzebul, in one form or another, seeks our loyalty. But we don't have to divide our allegiance. Quite the opposite! Fasting, which should make us weak, in fact strengthens us. Lent enables us to see more clearly the choices that confront us. Our lenten almsgiving assists us in getting free of the things that encumber our lives, things that divide our loyalty between God and money, between God and possessions. This gospel passage today encourages us to seek unity of purpose within our souls and harmony within our homes.

Lord God, too often I don't think of you as having any humor at all. When it comes to religion, I become very serious. Your word should serve as an example of that other part of you, the part that teases and cajoles us. All too often I just feel that you are threatening me. Help me to see the many ways you pull us more deeply into the mystery of faith. Enable me to laugh more at life and at myself, but always to be of one mind in serving you. Amen.

Friday of the Third Week

Hosea 14:2–10 • Psalm 81 • Mark 12:28–34

Return to the Lord!

Thus speaks Hosea. And Isaiah. And Jeremiah. And Jesus. Sometimes the readings of a season begin to sound like music in our ears. We begin to notice a certain repetition, of words, themes, and ideas. Lent does that to us—on purpose. All the lenten readings circle around a central theme: return to God! They all tell us, in one way or another, that during these 40 days we should focus our energies on turning back to God.

The readings also tell us how to accomplish that noble goal. Today, once again, we hear about commandments. Now, commandments aren't very popular these days. The world prefers to speak about "policies," but we all learn soon enough that this is another way of saying "commandment." Only God is direct enough not to skirt the issue. From the beginning, God has shown that there are certain expectations of us. "Let there be light!" That was a commandment, not a suggestion. God said, "Be fruitful. Multiply! Fill the earth. Subdue it!" From the beginning, God made it clear that there is work to do. And from the beginning, it seems, humanity has done its best to shirk its responsibility. That is why we need Lent. The ashes on our foreheads are like strings around our fingers, reminding us to do something: to return to the Lord, to accomplish the singular commandment of Lent.

Wise people understand this. Some folks are more fortunate than others and seem to know intuitively right from wrong, reasonable from unreasonable, good from bad. Others bump and clunk along through life, learning life's lessons the hard way. The Bible calls these people fools. The wise, on the other hand, seek God and seek goodness. The prophet Hosea reminds us of that today. He begins with the usual prophetic summons: Return to the Lord! He offers a few examples of foolishness and ends with the simple truth that those people are just who walk in the way of the commandments, along a path that leads without detours to God.

In the gospel, we meet a scribe, a learned man. He should be wise in the ways of religious teaching. He consults with Jesus about the way to God and about which commandments are worthy of our greatest attention. Jesus' response is interesting. He doesn't quote any of the Ten Commandments. Instead, he quotes a famous law from Deuteronomy: "Love God!" There is really nothing surprising about this, but the next sentence is. The second commandment, according to Jesus, is to love our neighbor as we love ourselves. Most of us do quite well at loving ourselves, so Jesus states a commandment—not a suggestion: to love others in the same way.

Lent is beginning to get really serious now! We have heard these ideas since Ash Wednesday, but today they are paraded before our eyes and souls as the essence of religion. If Hosea were around today, he would surely command us to "return to the Lord." He would also ask, "Are you wise enough to understand this? Are you faithful enough to do this?"

Lord God, your commandments are so direct and so simple, yet I spend so much time and energy avoiding them. Help me to listen to your commands with eagerness to fulfill them. Give me the strength and health to respond to my neighbor with compassion and concern, and may I keep making this Lent work for me by the way I follow your word. Amen.

Saturday of the Third Week

Hosea 6:1–6 • Psalm 51 • Luke 18:19–24

It is steadfast love, not sacrifice, that God desires.

These words are from the responsorial psalm of today's liturgy. It is a famous psalm, one of the seven "penitential psalms." The thought comes from the prophet Hosea. And Jesus. The words of the prophets are offered almost every day in Lent. Their words are frank and blunt, sometimes impolite, for truth often requires bluntness. Even though they may not fall comfortably on our ears, these words are often poetic, as in today's selection. What matters, though, is that their words are true and aimed directly at us.

The prophets understood what we don't; they saw things differently than we do. They saw life through God's vision of what could be, not our vision of what is. For this reason they always lived a little beyond their own time, even outside of time, and their words continue to have meaning.

Everyone thought that the gods of the ancient world wanted sacrifice. The more the better. The ancient Israelites thought that about their God too. It takes a prophet, someone who resonates with God's own insight, to offer a different view of things: that love is more important than sacrifice. That's the godly insight. The human insight, of course, is that much of the time it takes sacrifice to love as we should.

Hosea's description of God is both beautiful and frightening. Frightening because he tells the truth: God does come after us when we wander. Beautiful because Hosea reminds us of what we often forget: God also wishes to find us, not to punish us but to bring us home and to heal us.

The closing words of today's passage lead right into the gospel. Evidently Jesus was familiar with the teaching of

Hosea. He knew the words of the psalm, "It is love, not sacrifice, that God desires," and he was aware of God's desires. This parable, like every good parable, takes an old truth and teaches it in a new way. The old truth is the responsorial refrain: "It is steadfast love, not sacrifice, that God desires." The parable shows the meaning of this simple sentence.

It is easy to let religion become a "Sunday only" affair. We go to church, make a contribution, and then we go about the routines of our lives. So often churchgoers consider themselves superior to those who don't go, or to those who don't get as involved as they do, or to those who don't understand as much as they do. The Pharisee's error was certainly not in praying. That was good. The problem is that his own perception of what is acceptable to God and what is necessary to be religious excluded others from the inner circle. That happens easily in parishes, doesn't it?

The tax collector, on the other hand, had a different understanding. He knew his life's work offended people. There's nothing new in thinking that about tax collectors! But he saw that dealing with people was somehow connected with our dealings with God. Our Pharisee was blind to that; his vision was so narrow that he failed to see God in his neighbor.

The lesson is a good one for Lent, which wisely tells us to focus on prayer (God) and on almsgiving (neighbor). It's a hard balance and each of us must figure out for ourselves how to do it in our own lives. But, that is what Lent is for, isn't it?

Lord God, balancing life is difficult. There is so much to do and so little time. All too often I neglect the very people who love me. Or I get angry when their needs interfere with my finely calculated plans. Enable me to see all my neighbors through your eyes and to see others as fellow travelers along the way to the kingdom of God, not as obstacles. Help me, today, to be a good neighbor. Amen.

FOURTH WEEK OF LENT

"Laetare." Rejoice. That word has been connected for centuries with this Sunday of Lent. For four weeks now we have been observing this sacred season with our prayers, fasting, and almsgiving. We have been walking a little closer with Jesus and a little more carefully—and caringly—with one another.

Despite the discipline of Lent we have imposed upon ourselves, the church can never forget that the Lord is risen from the dead. This resurrection-presence of Jesus permeates us thoroughly, even in Lent. Maybe especially in Lent. Nonetheless, on this Sunday the church calls us to rejoice.

We can rejoice in the accomplishments of our Lent, no matter what they are. If they are not spectacular, if we have not been particularly faithful to Lent, then we can rejoice that there are still almost three weeks left to make the changes we need to make, to fulfill the promises we have made, to grow in faith. That fact alone, that God gives us such grace of time and hope, is sufficient cause for rejoicing.

In some places, rose-colored vestments replace the violet of Lent. Just for a day. The rose is a mixture of Lent's violet and Easter's white. No matter what the season of the liturgical year, it is still Easter that we celebrate in our liturgy. Perhaps today would be a good day to do something enjoyable: whether a special food, a good movie, or a visit, in person or by phone, to someone whose company we enjoy.

The fourth week of Lent will dawn with a whole new cast of characters in the daily readings. Often they are nameless, like strangers in a crowd. The stories this week will reveal tales of faithful followers as well as betrayers. The intensity of the season grows each day. Opposition to Jesus grows as well. In each day's reflections we are asked to take sides, for or against Jesus, for against a new way of understanding God's will and our lives. It is a week of honest but hard reminders. It will take some courage to face these words.

As this fourth week opens, let's review our progress. In regard to prayer, have we been reading Scripture? Not just the daily readings, but making our way through other books as well? Have we been reading anything besides the newspapers? Some good novels? Some books on spirituality or other Catholic literature? Have we taken time to go to daily Mass?

In regard to fasting, is the money we are saving on ourselves being given away to some needy cause? (I always find that Lent and Christmas are times that Catholic charities know enough to remind us of their need.) Have we made a donation to a local food pantry? Have we prepared something that we know others enjoy?

In regard to almsgiving, how generous have we been? Really! Lent usually finds us preparing our taxes too. What do our expenses reveal about our lifestyles? Is there something here that should change too?

It is the halfway point of Lent. May the measure of God's love help to fill the rest of these lenten days with spirit-filled growth, deeper faith, calmer hope, and listening hearts as we move together through another week of God's word to us.

Fourth Sunday of Lent
Year A

1 Samuel 16:1,6–7,10–13 • Ephesians 5:8–14
John 9:1–41

I cannot even imagine what it must be like to be born blind. It is beyond conjecture. I know that most seeing people, at some point or another, put on a blindfold for a game or will shut their eyes and pretend they do not see, but they always know that the blindfold will come off or that by just opening their eyes again, they will see.

These readings are about seeing and not seeing, about what seems obvious but in fact is hidden. They are wonderful readings that deserve a lot of time, reflection, and faith.

The first reading takes us back to the time of King David. Our destination is Bethlehem, not because of Christmas, but because that is the family home of David. Samuel, that man of powerful words and deeds, is seeking to anoint a new leader of Israel, a new messiah/king because Saul, the present king, had failed God. Jesse, according to the custom of the time, assumed that God wanted his eldest son to be the new messiah. He was wrong. The human tendency, of course, is to judge on external appearances, on what seems customary or obvious. But God, whose ways are different than our own, had other plans. God chose the youngest of Jesse's sons, David. Such a choice must have confounded Jesse and his older sons.

Even Samuel did not see things as God did. What was obvious to God was hidden from Samuel too. He lived in his own kind of darkness. His eyesight was fine, but his vision of God's will was clouded.

There are other characters in these readings whose vision is clouded: the man born blind, the disciples, the Pharisees, some parents, and undoubtedly, some of us. Again, our lenten readings ask us to put on the garb of these gospel characters and discern what part of them looks back at us in the mirror.

Sometimes we play the role of disciples in this gospel story. We ask questions and seek understanding. We look to Jesus for answers to the ultimate questions of life: Why are things the way they are? Whose fault is it that the man was born blind? Whose fault is it that evil has entered my life and has a grip on me?

Sometimes we are the crowd. We squabble over different opinions and shatter our relationships with others over who is right and who is wrong. We foolishly bring all kinds of darkness into our lives.

Sometimes we are the parents of the man born blind. We don't want to get involved and prefer to play it safe. We are so afraid and this paralyzes our love. Better to let someone else do it, we think.

Sometimes we are the Pharisees. We are so near-sighted that we don't see Jesus right in front of us. Or we are so far-sighted that we think only of heaven and forget about the people in front of us whose needs are very real today. Unwilling to change, we resist the initiatives Jesus is making in our lives. Instead of celebrating someone else's good fortune—like a man born blind who can now see—we criticize the intentions and deeds of others. Selfishness is a terrible darkness.

Sometimes we are the blind man himself. We can see with our eyes, but miss God's Spirit. We don't see the suffering that we cause. We don't see God's beautiful image in others. We are blind to the goodness that surrounds us.

Sometimes, too, we are Jesus. We can be light. What ultimately mattered for the blind man was not sight, the ability to see things, but insight, the act of faith that let him see Jesus, who shared his own light with him.

Every one of us can find ourselves in this story. Which character have you been lately? We bump into a lot of obstacles in life because of our blindness. This gospel reminds us that whenever we feel lost or confused or in need of light and insight, we should remember this gospel and the one who said, "I am the light of the world."

Questions for Reflection

1. Which of these characters most describes me this Lent? In what way? What can I do about changing?

2. We live in times that make it safe to be just "part of the crowd." In what way do I let anonymity protect me? Or let the crowd inhibit me?

3. What light do I have to share with the world (my family and friends, my parish or neighborhood) that I have been keeping to myself?

4. What do I see in my neighbor? A blind person who needs my guidance? an enemy? a stranger?

Fourth Sunday of Lent
Year B

2 Chronicles 36:14–17,19–23 • Ephesians 2:4–10
John 3:14–21

> "In the beginning God created the heavens and the earth. The earth was without form and void, and darkness was upon the face of the deep; and the Spirit of God was moving over the face of the waters." (Genesis 1:1-2)

Haunting, familiar words begin our reflection today. These opening words of Scripture pull us back to the primordial experience of God, into the unknowable origins of our world and of ourselves. We are pulled back into time and into the realm of mystery, where the Spirit of God hovers over the waters of chaos, and where nothingness threatens to rule. What does primordial darkness look like? What does Spirit look like? What does a shapeless world look like? Eerie, these beginnings of ours. This timeless vast darkness returns each evening, the realm of mystery and intrigue. Out of the silent darkness emerges a voice: God shaking apart the power of the darkness and commanding it to yield to light.

"And God saw that the light was good." God spoke in the darkness and the darkness scattered. It surrendered to the stronger power of light, which conquers the chaos, which shows things for what they are, and which reveals who we are. Darkness and light wrestle each other every day and in these middle days of Lent the light is gaining strength.

Lent flashes before us all the darkness of history: of Abraham's long dark night of the soul, obeying God's command to sacrifice Isaac, his only son; the darkness of the Hebrew people's slavery and God's call to them to live in the light of the commandments. Each dawn renews our hope and trust in the light, in God.

This remarkable third chapter of John's gospel begins in darkness. Nicodemus comes to Jesus at night. Knowing too well the darkness in which he lives, this leader of the people is afraid of being seen. What will people think? He uses the protective cloak of darkness to seek the light of the world.

Once again God speaks in the darkness, this time through Jesus. In the darkness of ignorance, Nicodemus ponders who this Jesus really is. Jesus' answer is startling: "Be born again!" Out of the darkness of confusion Nicodemus asks: "How can this happen?" Jesus responds: "By water and Spirit." Like the first creation, the New Creation in Christ is wrought in water and spirit. Nicodemus speaks for us all when he questions Jesus, who answers in simple, direct terms. The truth is this: This world no longer needs to reel about in darkness. Its light has come. The Son of God saves the world and condemns no one. No one.

In baptism's water and spirit we enter into the light of Christ, into the covenant community, the church. In the Eucharist we share the sacrifice of Christ, we share the covenant meal that guarantees our eternal life. Just as each dawn renews the power of light over darkness, so each Lent prepares us to celebrate the Easter Vigil, that night of light when Christ's power and love conquer death and darkness. Only in this gospel does Jesus remind us of the lifting up of the bronze serpent that healed the people of Israel. Jesus too will be lifted up, first on the cross, then to heaven. All who look upon him will be healed of the darkness of sin, doubt, pain, and death. The only judgment Jesus makes is to respect our freedom and allow us to make the choice: to choose light or darkness, to come near to him or to run from him.

Nicodemus came to Jesus at night. Slowly, slowly, by listening to the words of Jesus, Nicodemus came to understand, to see, and finally to believe. In the darkness of our own lives we too come to Jesus, a little afraid sometimes, a little hesitant because others might see how we are searching for the light of truth. It takes a lifetime to fully understand the depths of God's love. Slowly, slowly we come to understand the words, to see, to believe the mystery and power of these words of light: "Yes, God so loved the world that he gave his only Son, that whoever believes in him may not die, but may have eternal life." No more darkness. Only light. Life. New Creation. Christ.

Questions for Reflection

1. Do you know anyone in your parish's catechumenate (RCIA) program who is coming into the church this Easter? If you do, why not give them a call to encourage them? If you don't, perhaps you could call the Religious Education Office for a referral.

2. What makes us so hesitant about sharing our faith, talking about our faith? Why are we so much like Nicodemus, afraid someone might "catch" us being religious?

3. What parts of your life must Jesus illuminate this Easter?

4. What Catholic books or periodicals can you obtain to enlighten your faith and inspire your life?

Fourth Sunday of Lent
Year C

**Joshua 5:9,10–12 • 2 Corinthians 5:17–21
Luke 15:1–3,11–32**

What a story! The words strike deeply into our experience and into our souls. Some rename this parable "The Forgiving Father." Perhaps we should call it "The Lost Sons," for both treat their father shamefully. We all know the special pain of family rifts: anguish over ungrateful children, worry over siblings whose physical and emotional brutality to each other causes sadness and alarm. No one expects such things at birth, but the parable is clear about what is possible. Terrible family problems are not a modern phenomenon. They date back to Cain and Abel.

The Palestinian setting helps us to understand just how despicable each son truly is. A father might divide his property before his death, giving one-third to a younger son, but to ask for that share when the father is alive was unheard of, a scandalous act that manifested selfishishness and ingratitude beyond imagination. It is a death-wish against the father. Truly, this son is lost! The older son is equally shameful. He should have been a mediator between the other two, yet he doesn't speak a word, not against his brother or for his father.

Most fathers would bellow out their protest and anger at the son, punish him, and put him in his place. Not this father. He fulfills the request. Both sons are lost and family unity is shattered. This adventurous youth not only cuts himself off from his family, but in these small villages, everyone would soon learn of his actions and of the father's shame.

The spendthrift son wastes no time and quickly travels to a faraway place. There he squanders his fortune. His luck changes. Away from home, he is alone and hungry. No one cares about him, not even enough to give him some carob pods, the bitter berry that pigs uproot for food. Then, in this distant place, something remarkable begins to happen. His soul turns around inside him. He changes. He repents. He sets off on the road home, a symbol of his transformation.

The return will not be easy. How will his father respond? How will the townsfolk react? Before reaching his father's estate he must pass through the village where memory of his callous behavior will not be overlooked. He has failed and everyone will know it. Public humiliation will be his penance. Even if his father accepts him back as a servant, the villagers will not be so generous.

Again this father's actions were unusual. To save his son from public humiliation he runs out to greet the boy. The father further humbles himself, for no adult in the Middle East would run in public. He offers him the best robe, surely his own, as a sign of favor. He embraces and kisses him, a sacrament of reconciliation and forgiveness. Before the villagers can utter a scolding word, they are invited to celebrate. One lost son has returned home. As good as dead in society's eyes, he is fully alive, fully restored, has lost nothing, and has won back his own soul.

But the older son is still lost. The villagers found their way to the father's house, but not this son. He should have joined in the celebration as a gracious co-host, but again he does the unexpected. His reluctance is strange and foreboding, a key to his character. His complaint should have been reserved for private discussion, not public display: "I have slaved for you . . . you gave me nothing." He is as rebellious as his brother.

But both sons are loved . . . as we are. God reaches out to all of us, as different as we are one from the other, like these two brothers. One's public sin and another's private thoughts are both fair territory for God's all-embracing love. Both are reconciled at the cost of the father's humiliation, like reconciliation by a cross. It is a parable of unbounded grace, grace unfettered by any conditions whatever.

Perhaps nothing should be said about this parable. Perhaps we should just hear it and determine which role we play. That is the message of the parable and the message for Lent. We do not know how that older son responded. Did he repent? Did he change? He was forgiven and loved nonetheless. Do we repent? Do we change? We call these words the gospel, the good news, because we too are forgiven and loved nonetheless.

Questions for Reflection

1. Which role do we play this Lent?
2. Why is forgiveness so difficult for some people? for us?
3. Whom do we need to forgive before Easter? Why? How?
4. Is there someone, some situation close to us, that we should mediate (reconcile) in preparation for Easter?

Monday of the Fourth Week

Isaiah 65:17–21 • Psalm 30 • John 4:43–54

The man put his trust in the word Jesus spoke to him.

What was it like before creation? Genesis tells us that the spirit of God hovered over the primordial waters. Our beginnings are shrouded in mystery, perhaps in silence. What would such absolute silence be? We'll never know. Genesis then tells us that a sound broke the silence: "God spoke." God's word penetrated the void and creation began. We don't know if the speaking from God was a thunderous command or a wish in a whisper. We only know that when God spoke, everything began. Sun, moon, stars, light, birds, fish, cattle, and humanity all obeyed the summoning voice of God.

Isaiah teaches us that creation will take place a second time, a new creation. This time we know that there will be plenty of noise: the howling of winter winds, the thundering of cars, the roar of airplanes, the crying of babies, the whining of complainers, all the noise of technology—the earth will be filled with noise, so much noise, in fact, that it will be harder to hear God's voice. But God will re-create. Isaiah tells us that God wants to re-fashion the world, the same heavens and earth of Genesis, into a place of joy and delight. The ancient Israelites trusted that God would do this, that God would be faithful. Their trust paid off, because out of the misery of their exile, God re-created for them a world in which their faith developed.

That is why God sent Jesus. In the beginning of John's gospel, the gospel we are reading today, John calls Jesus "the Word." Jesus is God's Word, God speaking to us to help our faith grow, to re-create us. God sent Jesus, the Word, to speak words of healing, comfort, challenge, and hope.

The incident of the gospel is about words. A royal official knows well the power of words. His commands are obeyed, or else! How ironic that this powerful, influential man comes to Jesus, not to command him to act on his behalf, but to beg a favor. What a reversal of roles!

Jesus is returning from his ministry, from his God-speaking. Some people have listened; others have not. Now a royal official comes to him and listens. "The man put his trust in the word Jesus spoke to him, and started for home." This man, so accustomed to immediate results, had to do what everyone else has do to: trust God's word. This time the word created health; it turned sickness into health. Such power in a word! There is the point of this gospel: we too are summoned to put our trust in Jesus and in his word.

Lent is like that royal official. Lent asks us to seek out Jesus for our own healing, for the words that can create new life in us. Lent calls us to find the silence we need in order to hear this word. Lent also asks us to remove the clutter so that God's word will have a place in our lives and have its effect.

Lord God, you speak and everything happens. You speak and everything begins. Begin to speak to me, during this Lent, in my life. Let me quiet down all my busyness, so that I can hear your voice—in the words of the gospel, in the words of others, in the depths of my soul. Let me trust that your word will re-create me more and more in your image, healed of anything that prevents me from growing in faith. Amen.

Tuesday of the Fourth Week

Ezekiel 47:1–9,12 • Psalm 46 • John 5:1–3,5–16

There is a stream whose runlets gladden the city of God.

What an unusual phrase! Water and Jerusalem mixed together? Why is this psalm read today? It is because near Jerusalem's Temple Mount the ruins of the Bethesda Pool are resting under the stone ruins of Christian churches. The churches were built hundreds of years ago to commemorate this gospel. The whole area is honeycombed with channels and reservoirs that held the precious water used in biblical times for Temple ceremonies. These were the streams that flowed into the heart of the city of God, Jerusalem.

The popular legend was that once a day a messenger of God would stir up the water of this pool and the first person into the pool would be healed of whatever malady they bore. Imagine the daily chaos as people dashed to be first into the water!

Our nameless man, sick for thirty-eight long years, lived in the hope of a cure from God. Because of his affliction he was undoubtedly poor because he could do no work. He was poor too because in his mind his sickness was the result of sin. He was poor because he was alone, with no one to assist him into the pool. No one cared about him—until Jesus came along.

The myth of the pool's waters had no influence on Jesus. God's own strength and power was at work in him. The stream of God's grace was more important than the water of that ancient pool. Jesus singled out this lonely man and healed him, the one thing he needed. The man was obedient to Jesus' command. It was grace that healed him, not water.

Have you noticed how often Jesus uses the Sabbath to do

the holy thing, to help another? Yet, critics are many, then and now. Instead of rejoicing in the man's healing (imagine what it was like to finally walk!), Jesus' critics find fault with him for performing the wonder on the Sabbath. They miss the hand of God completely. That is hardly keeping the Sabbath holy.

Sad to say, the man misses it too. There are no words of thanks from him, none at all. Just the opposite, in fact. Despite his physical cure, he doesn't really know healing. He reports Jesus to the religious authorities, more worried about his standing in their eyes than with God. Perhaps he didn't like the brief lecture Jesus gave him about avoiding sin.

The man and Jesus met for the second time in the Temple precincts. The very water that he had sought for healing flowed into this area. Ezekiel knew the power of water to give life. We all do. In the ancient Middle East, where rainfall was unpredictable, water was nothing less than a grace from God. Ezekiel taught that one day these people wouldn't have to wait for the skies to open up. He taught that the life-giving water would flow from the Temple, from the source of true worship of God. No longer would the stream that flowed into the city gladden it. It would be the water that flows out of Jerusalem that will give joy and healing and life.

There's the next irony in these readings. In the very place where he should give thanks to God for the healing, the man betrays Jesus, as Judas will. As we move closer to Holy Week and Good Friday, our lenten readings will show us over and over again how the actions of Jesus will divide people into followers and betrayers.

Where do we stand at this midway point of Lent? How authentic is our worship? What healing do we still need? How do we respond to God's initiatives in our lives?

Lord God, your Son healed and comforted and taught. I like the healing and the comfort, but sometimes, like the man in this gospel, I prefer not to listen to the teaching. I like the miraculous, but prefer to avoid facing my responsibilities. Let this reading, with its reminder of the power of water, remind me also of my baptism, which I will renew at Easter. Let your water flow out of my public worship to renew the world and out of my private prayer to renew myself, healed of all sin and division, of all sorrow and doubt. Amen.

Wednesday of the Fourth Week

Isaiah 49:8–15 • Psalm 145 • John 5:17–30

"Whoever hears my word and has faith in God who sent me possesses eternal life."

This sentence is at the center of today's gospel. An author today might set these words off with bold print or italics. The ancient authors didn't have those devices, so they emphasized their ideas by the repetition of key words and ideas or set them in the center of their manuscript, as these words today appear.

As we move closer and closer to Holy Week, we will read this gospel of John more often. It is a wonderful gospel and worthy of hours of prayerful reflection. If anyone would read all of its chapters at a single time, some of John's key ideas would quickly become clear.

John begins his gospel by speaking about the eternal Word of God becoming flesh. He is writing about Jesus. God sent his Word to us in Jesus, a human being like us, so that we might understand more clearly the love and will of God. One teaching becomes clear throughout this gospel: God wants us to listen to his Word. It is as though the first word of Israel's great commandment, "Hear, O Israel, the Lord your God is One," is being brought directly into our human situation. In the gospels Jesus insists that those who are truly his disciples listen to him; when God speaks from the heavens (as at the baptism and transfiguration), God insists that we listen to Jesus.

That is part of our task this Lent: to evaluate how we listen to God's word, not just its comfort, but also its challenge.

"I solemnly assure you, whoever hears my word and has faith in God who sent me possesses eternal life." The next part of the sentence has two more major themes: faith and sending.

God sent Jesus as an emissary, a personal representative, to stir up our faith, our absolute trust in God's will and power to help, to love, and to save. Something very special, very human is taught about faith in John's gospel. Faith is not just a static assent to a list of teachings. It is more complicated than that, and more human. In this gospel, faith is clearly presented as a process that takes place deeper and deeper in our souls when we let Jesus enter our lives and speak to us.

Last of all, this gospel speaks about life and eternal life. We all tend to measure life in terms of quantity: days, weeks, years, and so on. Also, our culture reinforces this idea—that to be "really alive," we have to wear certain clothing and drink certain beverages, and so on. The Bible, on the contrary, is very consistent on this: to be really alive is to be alive in God. If we come into that circle of faith, drawn into it by hearing God's Word and by belief in Jesus, the qualities of eternal life are already ours. There is no waiting.

"I solemnly assure you, whoever hears my word and has faith in God who sent me possesses eternal life." This is the life of Easter: faith life, life in the word of Jesus, commitment to Jesus that brings life out of death, life not just in the distant future, but today.

Lord God, I often look to the future and overlook the present. You are present in both. May I grasp that I already share in your life because of my baptism. Help me today to see the new ways to share in your life by listening to your word, by following the example of your Son, and by loving my neighbor. Amen.

Thursday of the Fourth Week

Exodus 32:7–14 • Psalm 106 • John 5:31–47

"You are unwilling to come to me."

Old habits die hard. We all know that. Whenever some routine has become a significant part of our daily lives, it is difficult, threatening even, to change. If this is true about the activities of our daily lives, it is even more true about what we believe. Take, for example, Vatican Council II. The documents of the council asked the entire church to have a change of heart, to look at a new way of doing some things and a new way of thinking about our Catholic identity. For many people, this was very welcome; for others, it was incredibly difficult. We still live with the ambiguities of what that council really means in our church. Change is difficult.

Moses learned this in the desert with the Hebrews. For generations these people had been slaves in Egypt, accustomed to Egyptian ways, ruled by the expectations of the Pharaoh. When Moses encountered God at the burning bush, he knew that the people would be unwilling to follow him. He would need the name of God as proof. Later, in the exodus from Egypt, the people would question the wisdom of Moses in undertaking this flight and doubt the power of this God. After the initial excitement of the escape, there was time to ponder the event, to ask the questions that the Passover Night left unasked. When Moses himself disappeared into the cloud, like a teacher leaving a classroom, all kinds of revolts took place. Mutinous thoughts were spoken and unmentionable viewpoints expressed. The Hebrew people were not so sure about God's identity or intentions. Fear and stubbornness were winning the day.

Exodus also teaches that God is more changeable than the

Hebrews were, even than we are. When they built the golden calf, God had determined to rid the world of this ungrateful people, but Moses interceded and God changed the plans. Even when we are unwilling to go to God, God comes to us!

The Hebrew people learned over the centuries that their God was gracious, loving, forgiving. They remembered the acts of Moses in the desert and the word of Moses became the law of the land. When Jesus came, with other insights into the meaning of that law and its demands, these particular descendants of those who fled Egypt proved unwilling to listen to new words, to integrate his ideas into their experience of God. Old habits die hard.

It is Lent. This time of forty days begins with the summons to change. But halfway through Lent we are asked to look closely to see how well we are doing. How have we changed our ungodly patterns of activity and belief? How willing are we to believe what Jesus is saying? How willing are we to change? Even when we find it difficult to approach God, through fear or laziness, God keeps coming at us: in Jesus. In Lent.

Lord God, day after day you remind me of your power, always used for my benefit. On this Thursday of Lent, help me to come to you with joy, not fear; to come to you with honesty and integrity; to do what is necessary to straighten out the path that leads to the life you want to give me. Amen.

Friday of the Fourth Week

Wisdom 2:1,12–22 • Psalm 34 • John 7:1–2,10,25–30

"The truth is . . . he sent me. . . .my hour has not yet come."

Know. Send. Hour. Three simple words, but filled with meaning for this gospel. Once again, we confront ideas that are so central to the teaching of John's gospel that they are repeated again and again in order to keep them before our eyes.

Our Liturgy of the Word is beginning to prepare us for the climactic events of Holy Week. The poignant passage from Wisdom speaks the terrible truth that bad people seek to prey on good people, that evil cannot tolerate goodness and so it seeks to eliminate it. It is no surprise, then, that Jesus' enemies are beginning to plot to do away with him. Life for Jesus has become precarious.

Jesus knows this, of course. We all have an inner sense that certain decisions or actions will not be popular, understood, accepted. In this gospel, "to know" and "not to know" are pitted against each other. The leaders who think they know everything are the ones who really don't understand at all. They cannot "know" Jesus because their hearts and minds have been closed to him from the beginning. That is why they seek to kill him, to get rid of the one who challenges their authority and security with the truth.

A true follower can know Jesus; the genuine disciple seeks to learn truth not just to proclaim his or her own version of it. Jesus' truth is that he has come from God, not just from Nazareth. Anyone open to the truth comes to believe this.

"Send"—another key word in this gospel. Today we send faxes, e-mail, telegrams—technology unthought of in the ancient world. When an important person wanted to communicate a message to someone at a distance, a messenger would memorize the message and deliver it in person. It was expected that the trusted messenger would be treated with respect, as though the important sender was there in person.

Jesus is God's messenger to us. Even if the hearers in Jesus' time did not like his message, a certain respect was in order. Here, that protocol is lacking. In that ancient Mediterranean world, this is a terrible insult, to the sender and to the messenger. Jesus is faithful to the Sender, to God. Who better to deliver the message than Jesus, who knows God?

The last word is "hour." We all have significant moments, times that change the course of our lives. That is what Jesus refers to in this gospel. His hour is nothing less than the time of his death, resurrection, and ascension, the events that will forever change Jesus and us. That was why Jesus was sent into this world, the special intervention of God in history.

We share in that hour at our baptism when we are immersed into the death and resurrection of Jesus. Lent brings us slowly back to Easter, to the holy water that reminds us of our own moment of truth when we acknowledge that we know God, that we believe, and that we are willing to share in the ministry of helping others to know Jesus.

There can be much opposition to taking our baptism seriously. Even the best intentions are misunderstood, unappreciated. Then we need to turn to this gospel and remember that Jesus experienced those same feelings and frustration. But he didn't give up. He kept on doing what he was sent to do. So can we.

Lord God, you sent Jesus as your representative, as a sign of truth and love. I try to hear his word and respect his message. I do this in prayer and in my charity. Help me to see the way you send others to me, to help me on my journey to your kingdom. May I also see how you send me to others, to help them. Amen.

Saturday of the Fourth Week

Jeremiah 11:18–20 • Psalm 7 • John 7:40–53

"Look it up!"

Those are the words of a good teacher, someone who wants a student to learn how to learn. When we want to learn about Jesus, we look it up in our Bibles or in our catechisms, or in the wisdom of those who know him, but ultimately we must answer for ourselves, as each group does in today's gospel.

Who is Jesus? In the long run of life, this is the question everyone must answer. Everyone must decide. What role does he play in my life? What does Jesus have to do with me?

In the various encounters with Jesus that make up our gospels, everyone has to decide who Jesus is. The blind, whom he cures. The sick, whom he heals. The dead, whom he raises—all rather spectacular moments. Today the gospel offers us a more sobering example, the kind of decision that racks people's minds and tears at their souls.

So often it seems so clear to us, who this Jesus is. Most of us have grown up with Jesus, heard about him all our lives. When we feel that secure about Jesus, we stop looking things up. Yet everyone must make the final decision about what role he plays in our lives. Imagine how much more complicated this was for the people who were his neighbors, his relatives, the crowds who followed him. They had no New Testament to turn to. They had no "Jesus tradition" to rely on.

We see the debate in this gospel, an angry one at that. The gospel introduces the crowd, nameless people making decisions about Jesus, about who he is and where he comes from. Some consider him a prophet; a few others are more deeply moved, more convinced that he is indeed the messiah. With intentional irony, John shows us that the very people who should have been the first to recognize Jesus, the religious leaders, were the very ones who opposed him. Why? They thought they knew the answers.

How did he threaten them? Was it because he was a layman? Not properly educated, yet incredibly knowledgeable about God? Was it because he came from rural Galilee and not from the aristocratic ranks of the Jerusalem nobility? Was it because his charismatic leadership outshone the staid sophistication of the religious establishment? Was it all of these reasons?

The priestly class never seems to get along with Jesus. In all of the gospels, they are clearly enemies. In this gospel, the Pharisees join ranks with them, ridiculing anyone who begins to see God through Jesus. They belittle his followers, sweeping them aside with words of dismissal: "They are lost anyway!"

Only one leader defends Jesus, Nicodemus, who came to him under cover of night. He alone speaks up for an honest evaluation of Jesus. The others are so convinced that Jesus must fit into their old categories of religion and theology that there is no room in their souls for change.

There's that word again, change—that lenten word that calls us to be open to the new initiatives God is making in our lives. The world will always oppose change; its vested interests demand that. Good theology will always demand openness to new understandings of truth, of what God is doing in our world. What a pity when one group feels so threatened that it must insult the other and close itself off to the very grace that God wants to shower upon its members.

Our lenten fasting empties our stomachs, but we also need to empty ourselves of any sort of narrow-mindedness or smug security about our faith. The temple guards of this story tell more truth than their educated bosses. They say, "No one has ever spoken like this before!" They speak the truth, God's truth. We need Lent to hear it all over again.

Lord God, Lent moves into my life in surprising ways. I do change, sometimes despite myself. Lent also shows that I can grow, that I can let Jesus and my faith challenge me. On this day when the readings tell us how close-minded some people can be, open my mind to your revelation. On this day when the readings narrate how they made fun of Jesus and those who believe, help me not to worry about what others think of me, but to persevere in faithfulness. This I ask through my Lord, Jesus. Amen.

FIFTH WEEK OF LENT

Lent is quickly slipping away from us now. Already the fifth Sunday of Lent is upon us. Something remarkable happens in this week. For one, in all three years of the cycle of lectionary readings for this week the church shifts our attention to the gospel of John. The words of this gospel do not occur Sunday after Sunday in the three-year cycle, as do Matthew, Mark, and Luke's; they are always reserved for those occasions the church wants us to take most seriously. The very fact that the priest will announce on each fifth Sunday of Lent "A reading from the holy gospel according to John" should make us sit up straighter in the pew and listen more attentively.

Why this emphasis on John's gospel? Scholars remind us that the entire gospel of John is like watching a courtroom scene. Even though it appears that Jesus is the one on trial, the reality is that he has been sent by God to judge the world. In episode after episode this week, we become witnesses, bystanders, of the events that lead to Good Friday and Easter Sunday. We are privileged to overhear and witness the events that brought about Holy Week. It all begins this week.

In each day's account, the enemies of Jesus will try to consolidate their power over him. Jesus, of course, knows what is happening and even provokes his assailants with words—not weapons. He was sent to reveal truth, especially the truth that shows all of us for who we really are in the light of God's word.

This is a week that calls us to decisions. In the Bible, that is what "judgment" means: to make a choice, to decide. Our decisions will be for Jesus or against him. Our actions often reveal the decisions we have made about our faith and religion. That is another reason for Lent; we need this 40-day retreat to rethink things, especially the wrong decisions we have made. We need time to fix the damage we have done to others and to our own souls.

This week of Lent is a tough one, but that's all right. Our lenten discipline of fasting, prayer, and almsgiving should have made us a little tougher.

In this fifth week of Lent, you might want to consider:

Prayer. Find time to read the whole gospel of John. Look closely at the characters and determine which ones are most like you. If you haven't had the chance to attend a reconciliation service during Lent, you might want to do it this week. Many churches will not have them after Palm Sunday.

Fasting. A final effort to make this tough part of Lent work might be in order. Is there some agency that could benefit from your sacrifice of clothing, money, or food?

Almsgiving. The characters in the gospel this week who seek to kill Jesus are concerned with their positions and their influence. In our own society, we tend to judge people by what they have. This week, make a donation (the amount isn't all that important) to some cause you respect. If you are parents, talk with your children about "giving, not taking." You might give some of your time as well. Call your parish and ask if any special help is needed to prepare for Holy Week.

Fifth Sunday of Lent
Year A

Ezekiel 37:12–14 • Romans 8:8–11 • John 11:1–45

The pilgrim was a spindly old fellow with a staff, a basket hat, a brushy beard, and a waterskin slung over one shoulder. He was chewing and spitting with too much relish to be an apparition, and he seemed too frail and lame to be a successful practitioner of ogreism or highwaymanship.*

The story goes on to say that this pilgrim claimed to be the last Hebrew, a man who spent his years doing penance and waiting for the Messiah. He claimed to be 3290 years old and was looking for someone who had shouted at him once: "Come forth!" He said the man who shouted had told him to wait, and so he did. So he does. Wait. And look for that man who shouted at him.

The story is taken from a wonderful, haunting book, *A Canticle for Leibowitz.* It is set in the distant future. The old man is Lazarus, the central character of this gospel. He is waiting for the messiah, the one who shouted "Come forth!" to him. You see, it appears that Jesus forgot all about old Lazarus after this gospel episode and the poor fellow couldn't die again. All he could do was wander through the centuries.

It's a rather clever twist to the biblical story. We shouldn't be surprised at this. All during Lent we have been bumping into some rather strange characters in the readings. There was Abraham, who wanders. There was Moses, who wanders. There was Elijah, who talked with Jesus on a mountain. There was the woman at the well, who met a tired, thirsty Jesus.

---

* Walter M. Miller, Jr. *A Canticle for Leibowitz* (New York: Bantam Books, 1959), p.2.

There was the blind man, who demonstated all our spiritual blindnesses.

In each of them we see part of ourselves, believing yet questioning, always on the road to God, yet bumping into all kinds of obstacles. In the gospel today, it happens again. Martha and Mary feel that Jesus has forgotten about them in their time of need. Yet, though puzzled and hurting—perhaps even angry—they remain confident in him. The disciples certainly get in the way; they are filled with objections and don't understand. There's the crowd too. Wherever Jesus goes, the crowd follows. Crowds always follow, safely. At a distance, where it's easy to get away, where it's easy to remain anonymous.

Where are you in the story? In the crowd, perhaps? Curious about Jesus, but not really committed to him, your baptism still waiting to take hold? Perhaps you are a disciple getting in the way of others, trying to keep Jesus for yourself, not sharing your faith. Maybe you are like Martha or Mary, feeling that Jesus has forgotten you. Or maybe you just feel like Lazarus, dead to life, no energy, no trust in anyone, no faith in God.

No matter which character is walking around in your soul, Jesus enters the scene today with power and conviction. Mustering his divine energy, he looks right into your soul and shouts "Come forth to me, the source of life. Come forth and let me help you through life. It's me, Jesus. You don't have to wait for me. It is I who wait for you to come forward to let me untie whatever bonds are holding you prisoner. It's me, Jesus, waiting to roll away the stone that hides you from my sight, that hides you from God, that blocks your way to a rightful place in life."

Some time or other, each of those characters of the gospel story is part of us, walking around in us. No matter which one it is, Jesus says, "I am the resurrection and the life. I am. No other. My power can give you life. No problem of guilt is stronger than me. Even when you feel dead to God, to the world, or to yourself, if you believe in me, you will come to life. If you believe in me, you will never really die. Not in any way. Never."

Then Jesus looks deep into our own hearts and souls and asks us the same question he asked Martha and Mary, "Do you believe this?" What is your answer?

Questions for Reflection

1. What part of you this Lent is Lazarus, needing new life?

2. What part of you is Martha or Mary, interceding for someone else?

3. What part of you is the crowd, playing religion a little on the safe side?

4. Is there an acquaintance who needs your presence, your help, a share in your faith, before Easter?

5. How do imagine Lazarus felt at being raised from the dead?

Fifth Sunday of Lent
Year B

Jeremiah 31:31–34 • Hebrews 5:7–9 • John 12:20–33

"Christ gives us personality, personhood. The Incarnation teaches us how to be human beings in God's image. Christ has also given us God within, the constant and eternal Presence of his Love and his Being. Through Christ we are brothers and sisters; through Christ we are truly human, societal, and charitable; through him we find the meaning of suffering. We find peace amidst conflict, disharmony, hatred and oppression. Christ is God's peace. Christ is also God's love. . . .I can only thank God daily, and more than once, for having brought me into the center of his home [Roman Catholicism]."

These are the powerful words of a woman I met in Israel who works for Palestinian causes. Lynda emigrated from her homeland, South Africa, to Israel, where she gave up her native language and learned Hebrew. A Jew by birth, she is now a Catholic. Her words sound like those of a passionate theologian or the words in a potent sermon. They are the words of an intense woman who is dedicated to people because of Christ. They are the words of someone who has died to her past in order to come to life in Christ, who had to die to her personal history in order to become a New Creation. None of this transformation was easy for her, none of it fast. She understands today's gospel: "I solemnly assure you, unless the grain of wheat falls to the earth and dies, it remains just a grain of wheat. But if it dies, it produces much fruit."

Chuck was one of the more interesting students I have met. Not particularly studious, he was a character who loved mischief more than most students and was willing to pay the price when he got caught, which was most of the time. This penchant for mischief provided the courage Chuck needed to face other, more serious, risks. To be free from the cowardly cancer that ultimately claimed his 23-year-old life, Chuck had to conquer death and its power by facing it head on. During this time he wrote to me: "I learned a lot since I got sick. I don't really know how to explain it. I know that I learned a lot about people and about myself." This young man took the time to write about these insights when he could hardly move his hands. His words reveal a simple, strong faith, and show that he understood the meaning of his baptism. He, too, wrote that he understood today's gospel: "I solemnly assure you, unless the grain of wheat falls to the earth and dies, it remains just a grain of wheat. But if it dies, it produces much fruit."

Everyone knows stories like these. We have all been touched by remarkable men and women whose lives mirror this gospel and are living parables of Jesus. Sometimes they are the saints of our spiritual reading; other times, like Lynda and Chuck, they are closer to home. The grain of wheat must sacrifice its existence as a seed if there is to be a new shaft of wheat, a new form of life. God calls us again and again to sacrifice, to die to ourselves in order to come alive to others, to produce much fruit. We can do this because Jesus has done it first. Our tendency to hang on, to preserve the status quo, to have a no-risk existence is made null and void by our baptism, which is our entrance into a covenant with God to let God change us, to let God give us crosses, to move from the daily dying of our lenten practices to the eternal life of Easter.

During Lent the fields around my rural parish lie fallow, awaiting the spring seed. Rich dark clods of Wisconsin soil wait for the chance to yield the harvest of a new season. Just so, God waits for us during Lent to see how our fallow souls can come to life in Jesus once we give ourselves to Jesus and come to life for one another. Even the fields understand today's gospel: "I solemnly assure you, unless the grain of wheat falls to the earth and dies, it remains just a grain of wheat. But if it dies, it produces much fruit."

The strangers who come to the disciples at the beginning of today's gospel ask to see Jesus. We are more fortunate than they. We see Jesus wherever people gather to hear this word, to celebrate the victory of life over death, wherever people serve one another in memory of Jesus. Lynda and Chuck and the soil know where to look for Jesus. They know the meaning of the words. Do we?

Questions for Reflection

1. What people and their stories do you know about who serve as examples of this gospel? Can you contact them, talk to them, thank them?

2. Does our "American way of death" reflect a belief in the resurrection? That is, is death part of faith or part of tragedy?

3. When was the last time you planted a seed and watched it grow?

4. What sort of "witness" story can your life offer?

Fifth Sunday of Lent
Year C

Isaiah 43:16–21 • Philippians 3:8–14 • John 8:1–11

This morning the last remnant of winter, a crescent of ice, rested on the pond. Spring is late this year. The brilliant morning sun skittered across the pond's rippled surface as two geese stood on the ice and honked their displeasure with the imminent demise of winter. Their haven was slowly, gently disappearing from under them. For all they knew, the very foundation of the world was disappearing. One would think the geese had no escape from the inevitable, as though they had forgotten their wings. No wonder we call them "silly geese."

Our spring has had a hard time making its arrival this year. Last-minute snowstorms sneak up on us and make life sloppy and still a bit precarious. I suppose we should all be used to this, but we never are. We become so accustomed to everything that we forget how things can change. The weather changes; the world around us changes. Isaiah's words, it seems, are coming to life: "See, I am doing something new! Now it springs forth; do you not perceive it?"

Changes in ourselves, unlike changes in the weather, take time, certainly more than a season. Consider our task for Lent! For five weeks now we have been trying to change ourselves, trying to let God change us. How are we doing?

That's where we meet Jesus this week, changing things, changing expectations, changing the way we think about God's justice, changing the way we think about each other. We meet Jesus in the temple area, that magnificent esplanade of Jerusalem where the great teachers lectured and powerful leaders pronounced judgment and issued punishment.

Our gospel tells us that some of these leaders brought forward a woman who had been caught in sin. Like geese on the pond ice, those leaders strutted around protesting her action and demanding a decision from Jesus. What would he say? If he didn't join in the condemnation, they could accuse him of heresy, of not caring about the ancient law of Moses. If Jesus did join in the condemnation, then all his teaching about mercy would be hollow. A lesser person would have panicked, but not Jesus.

The sinless one and the sinner confront each other. In the background, the self-righteous chatter about them both. St. Augustine described this meeting: *misera et misericordia*—misery and mercy meeting, sin and forgiveness facing each other.

Any priest or minister can tell us about people whose lives are complicated by sin. These are people who seek reconciliation, who want to put their lives back together again. This gospel serves as a splendid model: in justice not to tolerate the sin, but in love to forgive the sinner generously. There is the lesson of the gospel. Jesus erases any false images of an angry God. The men who brought this nameless woman before Jesus were unforgiving. They had caught the woman and now they thought they had also caught Jesus. But Jesus is not so easily intimidated.

With incredible gentleness and clever words he frees the woman from her sin and at the same time exposes the self-righteous for what they truly are: the real sinners. Jesus must have smirked a bit when he asked, "Where did they all disappear to?"

For the third week in a row the gospel teaches about forgiveness. Also, for the third week in a row, we do not know if the main character of the gospel ever did change. Did the woman sin again? We will never know. But we do know how well we repent, how well we change. Not only does Jesus forgive, but his forgiveness is without judgment. He is strong in his opposition to sin, yet he is tender to the sinner. To us. His gentleness melts away our fear of God and of change. As we move together toward the end of Lent, this gospel serves as an invitation to let God change us, to let God forgive us, to help us forgive others, and to help us forgive ourselves.

Questions for Reflection

1. Is there some sin lurking around in your life yet? Have you taken advantage of the sacrament of reconciliation this season?

2. Once on this Sunday, a young man who had vandalized our church came to make a public apology to the congregation. How marvelous an experience: once he entered the church under cover of darkness, a coward. This day he entered in broad daylight, mustering the courage he needed to face the congregation. When he finished, the people applauded. Forgiveness on top of forgiveness. Is there anyone who needs your forgiveness? Is there anyone who needs to forgive you?

3. Is it possible to "forgive and forget"?

4. Given this gospel, what is your idea of the "final judgment"?

Monday of the Fifth Week

Daniel 13:1–9,15–17,19–30,33–62 • Psalm 23
John 8:1–11*

"I am completely trapped!"

Such readings! Such tales! Such human drama and divine intervention! Both these readings, minus the divine intervention, sound like the plot of a soap opera. There are beautiful women, lecherous old men, and righteous defenders of the helpless. Against overwhelming odds, in both stories, the righteous win. Truly, there has been divine intervention.

The first story is set in the mysterious east, in Babylon, during hard times. It is apparent from the start that Susanna is completely innocent. The men are evil, not Susanna. Evil intentions lead them to deceit and ultimately to death, which is where sin always leads: to death of the body, death of the heart, and worst of all, death of the soul. That is when we feel like saying, with Susanna, "I am completely trapped!"

In between the lines of the readings are the laws of ancient Israel, about coveting another man's wife, about the punishment for sexual misconduct, about desiring. In the beginning, Genesis tells us, it was desire that brought about the downfall of humanity. As soon as desire enters our minds, it works to control all of our faculties to get what it wants. Look at what those men were willing to do! It was desire that trapped them.

In the gospel we meet a similar experience. Once again men bring a woman forward accused of sin. In this story, there is no question about her guilt. She, too, is completely trapped. Isn't it odd that John never mentions how lecherous these men must have been to have caught the woman in the act of adultery! Notice, too, there is no mention of her accomplice in

*In Year C, John 8:12–20 is the gospel for the day.

the deed. The punishment for this offense, in the law of Moses, was stoning, hurling large rocks at the victim—a terrible death.

Jesus appears to be trapped too, doesn't he? If he denies the punishment decreed by Moses, he loses face and credibility with the crowd. If he consents to the punishment, all his teaching about forgiveness vanishes into the air. But Jesus' simple sentence to those who condemn, even when the punishment was legal, cuts into all our hearts: "Let the one without sin of their own cast the first stone."

It is easy to see the sin of others and condemn it, easy to be self-righteous instead of righteous. It is also easy to feel trapped by our situations in life or by our sin. As clever as these words of Jesus are, the deeper beauty of this gospel rests in the final words of Jesus to the woman, the simple command to avoid the sin. It frees us from the snares others set for us or those we foolishly walk into by ourselves. In this gospel we see again that boundless compassion spills out from God through Jesus to all of us. All the time. Thank God!

Lord God, so often I feel trapped by life, caught in situations beyond my control. Sometimes it has a lot to do with sin, in one form or another; sometimes it is just the way things are. Your Son sets us free from all those traps. Help me to see how I can be freed from my own sin and guilt and how I can help others to be free. All I need to do is to listen to the tender words of your Son: "Go, and from now on avoid this sin." (And by the way, help me stop throwing stones at others too!) Amen.

Tuesday of the Fifth Week

Numbers 21:4–9 • Psalm 102 • John 8:21–30

Because he spoke this way, many came to believe in him.

The love of my life is reading, studying, and teaching the Bible. It is not always easy, because the Bible is a complicated book. There is much to learn about it, and often students come to it with familiar, but strange, ideas about its meaning. One of the tools that I have found very helpful in studying the Bible myself and sharing that with others are large felt-tip markers.

I always suggest that students purchase a set of markers to highlight special words of the Bible. For example, in the gospel of John, there are several words that are repeated throughout the gospel. We see several of them in this passage for today. By highlighting repetitious words, the words begin to stand out, to get the attention that John wanted them to have. Our ears might hear the words, but it is always good to use our senses of touch and sight in addition.

In this passage "world" and "sin" dominate the conversation of Jesus. This wonderful world, with all its goodness and potential that God created and considered good, soon began to disintegrate. The Bible expresses the conviction that sin is responsible for this, so much so that before long the good world and the evil of sin began to merge. The two became one.

The world becomes the arena of our problems: relationships with other people, self-doubt and disappointment, suspicion and hurt and danger. All of this, John teaches us, is the sin of the world, which disorients us and leads us away from God.

Jesus was sent by the creator to set aright all those things that had gone wrong. Sin needed to be stopped cold in order to allow the people of God to get their bearings and continue their pilgrimage through life, to God. Jesus accomplishes this massive task by his fidelity to God's mission, by speaking the truth. "Because he spoke this way, many came to believe in him." At last, there was someone whose very word was as powerful as God's words of creation.

The other side of the story is the world around us. In a world accustomed to lies, truth is a challenge and a threat. There will always be those who prefer the way of lies, perhaps because it is more exciting or more profitable. Likewise, there will always be those who listen to Jesus, who are swayed by his example of truth, by his authentic way of living the goodness God desires for us all.

God's word always calls us to make choices, to choose between good and evil, between listening to Jesus and walking away, between the way of the "world" and the way of Jesus. By passing the words "world" and "sin" before our eyes, Lent clearly presents us with this choice. It summons us to make a choice about which of the two ways will have our allegiance, the word of the "world" or the word of God.

If all this gets confusing, that's understandable. This gospel tells us that some did not understand Jesus. But Jesus didn't give up on his audience and he doesn't give up on us. He continues to speak the word of God until our faith deepens, until our commitment is clear, until our faith is shored up. God did not desert Jesus, and Jesus does not desert us. Never.

Lord God, more and more I realize that Lent calls me to make decisions about what to do, whose word to believe, how to act. I know the world around me can be so good sometimes, so evil at others. Help me to make wise choices and always choose faith in your Son. Amen.

Wednesday of the Fifth Week

Daniel 3:14–20,91–92,95 • John 8:31–42

"The truth will set you free."

Truth—a simple word but a difficult reality. Jesus says that "the truth shall set you free." How different from Pilate's cynicism: "Truth—what is that?" Isn't that the way it always is, though? Jesus tells the truth. Jesus is the truth. That is the best description of truth: Jesus. Pilate and all the others like him prefer to define truth their own way. That way, they are never responsible. They can twist and turn the words to make them say what is "politically correct," what is acceptable to their bosses or to the crowds they seek to please.

Powerful people usually think that they can do that to the truth. That is not truth, however; it sets no one free. In fact, it makes us slaves to falsehood and lies. We see a good example of this in this first reading from the Book of Daniel. Nebuchadnezzar is the protagonist. The king of Babylon, he ruled one of the most powerful empires the world had ever seen. He had destroyed Jerusalem utterly, leaving it without a temple, without sacrifice, without a king. His name was to be feared and he could manipulate the truth to suit his policies.

One of the policies is the center of this reading: to worship a false god, an idol. Truthful people, those who believe in the one true God, cannot do that, worship something that is false, that isn't even there to begin with. But people have always bowed down before easier, more convenient truths, before less demanding gods. Only God's truth can set us free.

The heroes of our story cannot accept Nebuchadnezzar's version of truth. Three young men know the truth that the king of Babylon does not know. Despite threats to their lives, they do not yield. Most people yield considerably short of such a threat. Their faith is their salvation, for ultimately God will not allow lies to win. Nebuchadnezzar, the nemesis of Israel, by the end of the story comes to bless the God he does not even know or has ever experienced. Even he is capable of change, of conversion.

Not so the people in this gospel episode. They cannot bring themselves to trust the word of Jesus completely, to live according to his truth. Like the three young men in prison, Jesus is not intimidated, neither by their numbers, their accusations, nor their arguments. Each time he answers them he simply responds with more truth, and the crowd grows angrier. As they do, they move further from the very truth standing before them.

For some people, the word of Jesus that liberates is so different from the "truth" of the world. The world tries to enslave us by manipulating what we hear and see, how we see it, when we see it. The freedom—truth—that Jesus offers is so up-front and honest that the world cannot tolerate this threat to its power, security, or comfort, so it seeks to belittle that truth or those who preach it or accept it.

We all have a tendency to decide what is true and not true, to become fixed in our ideas, and so we close our souls to new words, new people, new possibilities, new ways of understanding the ancient truth of God's love. Lent comes along to shake us up, to remind us that the call to conversion is constant. If we want Lent to work, we have to let Jesus free us from anything that closes our minds to his word. "If you live according to my teaching, you are truly my disciples; then you will know the truth, and the truth will set you free."

Lord God, your truth is simple and straightforward. Help me to understand that. Let me see that when things begin to get complicated, it is usually lies that are its source. In this late week of Lent, enable me to choose your truth and to live by it, to choose your words and do them—to choose the way of your Son. Amen.

Thursday of the Fifth Week

Genesis 17:3–9 • Psalm 105 • John 8:51–59

"I keep his word."

Isn't misunderstanding the way of life for most of us? We try to communicate clearly, but there is always someone who misunderstands. They hear innuendo we don't intend. They miss words that give meaning to the other words. They hear what they want to hear, what they presume we are saying. Misunderstanding! How odd that this problem gets increasingly worse as our means of communicating become more sophisticated!

Jesus had only words, no machines. He spoke a word of truth and it was misunderstood. His enemies twisted the words, and even his followers often didn't understand his meaning. For some time now, in our lenten readings, Jesus has been speaking about his mission, his Father, and his identity. Despite the clarity, directness, and truth of much of what he said, many people misunderstood. "Who do you make yourself out to be?" they asked. Jesus has said quite clearly that he was sent from God, but his words were not the fiery words of revolution that most wanted to hear and they were not a blanket approval of religious practice that alienated people from God. His words were true and straightforward.

Abraham listened to God. He listened to the difficult command to leave home and move to a strange land. He also listened when he was told to sacrifice his only son, Isaac. And so God made a promise to be on the side of Abraham and his descendants. God would always keep that promise, that covenant with Abraham.

In the gospel today, John wants us to see how that openness to listening was lost, why these heirs of Abraham were not as open to new experiences of God as their famous ancestor. In front of them stood the promise-made-flesh, the word-made-flesh—Jesus.

The closer we move toward Good Friday in our lenten journey, the more tense the situation becomes between Jesus and the crowds. It becomes so tense, in fact, that the crowd is prepared to stone him. As we make our own way closer to that Week of Fire, we need to check ourselves too. We need to examine how well we are listening to the new words, to the new initiatives that God continues to communicate during Lent through the sacred word and through the One he sent to us, Jesus.

Are we open to God's word? Do we live according to it? Do we understand fully all that God does for us? All that God requires of us? Or are we like that crowd in the gospel that doesn't quite catch on? Do we understand? Do we? Really?

Lord God, from the beginning of Genesis you spoke. Your words brought life to the world, light out of darkness. Your words directed the patriarchs and matriarchs, the prophets and wise. Why, then, is it so hard to put my trust in your promises? May I listen with attentive ears to your word, to every nuance and syllable, like a love letter, trying to figure out every possible meaning. Help me, no, make me know your Word, Jesus. Amen.

Friday of the Fifth Week

Jeremiah 20:10–13 • Psalm 18 • John 10:31–42

"Many good deeds have I shown you from the Father. For which of these do you stone me?"

"This is the cup of my blood of the new and everlasting covenant." "Covenant" describes the relationship that exists between God and us. We hear the word at every Eucharist. It is the solemn agreement between God and us that God will take care of us. In return we are obligated to follow certain laws exemplified particularly by "Love one another."

Every Jewish person would know the word "covenant." It defines the relationship God made with the people in the desert at Mount Sinai. They would know, too, the obligations of the commandments God imposed upon them, and the "obligation" on God as a result of the covenant: "I will be your God."

There is another word that hovers between the lines of every covenant sentence: love. In the Old Testament, the Hebrew word is clearer: *hesed*. It describes the obligation that people have toward one another, to be on someone else's side, no matter what. That is the kind of concern that God has for Israel and for us. That is the love that Jesus keeps speaking about in his ministry.

Covenant love (*hesed*) consists of actions for others, good works such as caring for the sick, the lonely, the helpless, the confused, the hurting of any society, of any time, of any place. We might say that this is God's "job description." These are the activities that God does for us in covenant love.

Long ago, God sent Jeremiah to remind the people of their obligation to God and to one another to be faithful to the covenant. Jeremiah's mission was not easy. People did not want to be reminded of covenant obligations. Instead, they went after him, even his family and friends. They made his life miserable, as we see in this first reading, plotting against him to discredit him and finally to kill him. That was the reward for his fidelity to the covenant.

God sent Jesus to accomplish those same goals. Isn't that what the gospel continually describes: Jesus healing the sick, telling the truth, bringing light to the blind and confused, bringing forgiveness—not condemnation—to sinners, bringing life out of death. Jesus does the works of God, called "good works" in this gospel.

Everyone who saw these activities should have seen God at work in Jesus. But some didn't and that is why Jesus had to ask, "For which of these good deeds do you stone me?" Some see healing, kindness, forgiveness, and truth as threats. Such people will always try to eliminate that threat. These are the people who plotted to arrest Jesus in order to put him to death.

Their ancestors had tried to do the same thing to Jeremiah centuries before. Poor Jeremiah. All he did was tell the truth, but truth has powerful enemies. It also has more powerful advocates.

Throughout this gospel of John we see how those whose hearts are open to the word of Jesus come to believe in him. It takes time to figure out the difference between the influence of the "world" and the way of Jesus, but truth will win out.

By the close of this gospel Jesus has to flee Jerusalem, but many who had heard truth and wanted more sought him out. They had seen God at work in Jesus and wanted to hear more and be part of that work. They followed Jesus even to remote places to hear more truth about their God.

That is what Lent is about: growing in faith, wanting more of Jesus' life-giving love in our own lives. That way we can continue to do the good works, the covenant works, that mark us off as the people of God.

Lord God, how often I hear that word "covenant" without thinking about its meaning. I and all others are tied to one another in faith, but sometimes that is so intellectual. We also need to tie ourselves to one another in good works. Isn't that the meaning of religion? To tie ourselves, to commit ourselves, to you and to others? Let my good works increase in number and become more sacrificial as I move closer to that final sign of your covenant with us, Good Friday, only a week away. Amen.

Saturday of the Fifth Week

Ezekiel 37:21–28 • Jeremiah 31:10,11–12,13 (Response)
John 11:45–57

"If we let him go on like this, the world will believe in him."

Such opposite readings, a careful juxtaposition of messages and feelings! Ezekiel is almost in ecstasy reporting God's words outlining the wonderful life awaiting those who take God's covenant seriously. God will be in the midst of the people, recognized and honored, worshipped properly in the Temple.

How sad, then, by contrast to read the gospel episode. There is the Son of God, Jesus, in the midst of the people, unrecognized and unappreciated. The ungodly motivation of the religious leaders is especially appalling; they are afraid of the popularity of Jesus. "If we let him go on like this, the world will believe in him." The statement is filled with irony, for by the time John wrote it, the word of Jesus had indeed gone out to the whole world known at that time.

The effect of all Jesus had said and done was envy, not belief. Although Good Friday is still a long way off in the chapters of the gospel, it begins with these words, with Jesus fleeing from the very people he came to help.

The two readings offer us the same choice we have seen repeated during Lent. We can choose the way of the "world" or the way of God. The way of God is the way of baptism, of trying to be faithful to the example of Jesus, a way of life that is reflective, prayerful, and mindful of the needs of others. That was the example Jesus gave, that threatened the leaders. This way of life looks toward others' needs rather than self-interest. It is the way of God, the fulfillment of Ezekiel's vision.

The way of the "world" is the selfish, anxious way of looking at life and other people, a way of life that seeks rewards, possessions, status, and control over others. This way will always seek to belittle those who follow Jesus. It will always be suspicious of goodness, for there is no profit in it, and it will do everything it can, by innuendo or direct action, to stop the influence of Jesus from spreading.

As we approach Holy Week, we need to look again at our own way of life, to ask God's grace not to be tricked away from our baptism, to ask God's way to guide the decisions and actions of our lives.

We know from readings like this gospel that it has never been easy to be a follower of Jesus. We always live with one foot in each of those worlds. But even though the "world" might have heard the word, it still doesn't believe. Not completely. That is why we need Lent, to remind us of who we are and what we called to do because of baptism, the very baptism we will renew at the Easter Vigil, one week from today.

Lord God, seldom does your word jolt me as strongly as it does in Lent. These readings show that I am responsible for my actions, for my baptism and for my faith. For over five weeks now I have been listening to your word calling me home to you. Let my response reflect Ezekiel's exuberant joy, to place my trust in your word and to worship you in every way. Make me attentive to my own baptismal vows. May I ponder them carefully as I search for your life in my own. Amen.

HOLY WEEK

Holy Week is a week of fire, a week of danger, a week of awe. It appears to be just another week of days, but we believers always know that time is measured differently than the world measures it. And this week the world around us watches and wonders as we pause often from normal activities to pray. We pray to express our belief, to show who we are, and to offer thanks.

It is a week of awe because of what we do. So often at the end of a conversation we hear, "Have a good day!" I have often felt that this simple phrase is trite. It is, I believe, an empty wish for the most part, something people say because it is expected, like the predictable messages on answering machines. Good days do not fall out of the sky, ready-made. Rather, we make them good or bad, holy or unholy, by the way we respond to God's initiatives.

In Judaism, the cluster of holy days that include Rosh Hashanah (New Year) and Yom Kippur (The Day of Atonement) is often called the "Days of Awe" because in that span of time Jews observe many of their most sacred festivals, something similar to Holy Week, our days of awe. Nowhere else in the Christian calendar do we recall all the central mysteries of our faith in such a short period of time. From Passion (Palm) Sunday to Easter Sunday we stand in awe of what God has done for us and what we have done to God. Awe produces silence. In Holy Week we should be silent often, pondering the mysteries and finding our place in the crowd, whether in the crowd of Palm Sunday, or at the foot of the cross on Good Friday, or in the crowd of worshippers at our parish church during the week.

Holy Week is also a week of danger. The danger is twofold.

For Jesus, it was a troubled week. He knew well the consequence of not escaping the Garden of Olives when he had the chance. Danger lurked all about him, in soldiers and in friends. How could he even know friend from foe, betrayer from believer? In each day's readings we will hear of the increasing danger to Jesus and how he faced down his enemies and his own fear.

The week is also dangerous because of what it does to us. It changes us. This week finds us in church more often than usual; it finds us more reflective than usual. What would your boss, your children, your neighbors, your parents, or your spouse think if they could read your mind as you ponder the mysteries of this week, as you show up for public prayer in this week's ceremonies? As Lent ends, it is dangerous for others to see the witness of how much you might have changed and continue to change because of this week.

Finally, this week is a week of fire. It burns in our souls, our yearning for God. It is a fire of an early Pentecost, warming our faith to new levels. It is a fire that purifies, as we hear the passion accounts of the gospels and measure our lives against the life of Jesus. It is the fire of the Easter candle, that single flame brought into the church that brightens the building and the hearts of believers, the flame of faith that enables us to look into the tomb and to see that it is empty because Jesus fills our souls with his resurrection presence.

Fire. Danger. Awe. Holy Week. Our week of faith.

Suggestions for the Week

1. By all means, find out when the special ceremonies of the week are scheduled for your parish and plan to attend.

2. Call the pastor or liturgy director to ask if there is anything you can do to help them in this busy week.

3. Call a friend or relative who usually doesn't go to church and ask them to join you for one or all of these special days.

4. If your parish priest or parish director is living alone, offer to prepare some meals during this very busy week.

5. Take time to reread the readings of the ceremonies and perhaps "write" your own homily/reflection in your mind.

Passion (Palm) Sunday
Year A

Matthew 21:1–11 (Procession) • Isaiah 50:4–7
Philippians 2:6–11 • Matthew 26:14–27:66

This is the most familiar of gospels. We know it so well that we can repeat many of its verses from memory. The names, places, and the sequence of events are etched into minds and souls from the countless times we have heard these words, watched them in films, and pictured them in our minds.

For each of us, one or other aspect of the passion narrative is particularly significant. Each paragraph offers material for a lifetime of reflection, an abundance of truth, the full proof of God's love for us.

The final goodbyes at the Last Supper, the sleepiness from drinking the Passover wine and the need to pray in the garden, an illegal night trial, the soldiers' taunts, the last words—all mix human drama and divine pathos in a way that assures us of the holiness of this word, a guarantee of its truth. All of this speaks to our own experiences of betrayal and denial, of crosses feared and crosses carried, and of our hope that Jesus understands our struggles because of his own.

So many characters appear before us in the lengthy narrative of the passion that it is difficult to single out one for special attention. Each of us has that distinct passage or character that is especially significant to us, one we make our very own. This year I would like to present the character of Simon of Cyrene for your consideration.

Simon is certainly not at the center of the stage, is he? It is a coincidence—or the providence of God—that he gets involved at all. We know nothing about him, just his name, a common one at that. The Bible doesn't even tell us if he became a follower of Jesus. If ever someone was in the wrong place at the wrong time, it was Simon. Or perhaps, if we look at this with the eyes of faith, he was just where God placed him. Aren't we all?

The Romans often forced innocent bystanders to work for them, to carry their equipment, to run unpleasant errands. It was always safer to avoid the Roman soldiers. This day Simon didn't. His mistake. Jesus talked about this custom in his Sermon on the Mount. He said that "if anyone presses you into service for one mile, go for two miles!" The same word is used here to describe what Simon does for Jesus. He is pressed into service. He was forced to carry the equipment of death, the cross. Simon, the innocent bystander, unwittingly and unwillingly becomes involved in this momentous event.

What Simon did is commemorated in Jerusalem at the Fifth Station of the Cross. Al-Wad (Valley Street) still runs from the Damascus Gate to the Temple area. It is always crowded with pilgrims and shoppers. Perhaps Simon was among the Passover visitors to Jerusalem that day. Perhaps he was in the city to make a last-minute purchase before Sabbath began. The Via Dolorosa (Way of Sorrows) makes a sharp turn to the right at this Fifth Station, leading up a narrow, stepped street. This is where visitors get confused and have to ask directions. Perhaps Simon paused here and his hesitation led to the soldiers' summons to help.

Did he want to help? Did he want to get involved? Did he know Jesus? Did he even know about Jesus? We don't know, but we do know that he did what Jesus told his followers to do: go the extra measure without hesitation. The disciples had long since fled; they were not around to help carry the cross. All those who had heard the wonderful words of the Sermon on the Mount were gone, and a stranger is left to fulfill the instruction of Jesus.

In many ways we all look for a Simon of Cyrene, for someone to carry our burdens, to do our work for us. The first reading of this Sunday liturgy speaks poetically about the Servant of the Lord, a solemn reminder that all are called to service, even to carry crosses. The wonderful song in Paul's letter to his beloved Philippians tells the same truth: believers follow the example of Christ, humble service to others, no matter what the cost. So often it is other, nameless people who pay the price for our comfort, who suffer for our sins.

Simon of Cyrene did these things. We read of no objection or question on his part. He just did what he was bidden. We who believe are called to do the same: take care of others, serve humbly, and go the extra measure with Jesus.

Questions for Reflection

1. When was the last time you had to do something you really didn't want to? What was the task? How did you respond to the call for help?

2. Whom do you go to for spiritual help in your life? For emotional help? Who is your helping neighbor?

3. Which character in this familiar gospel reading do you find particularly fascinating? Why?

4. If you could "freeze frame" some episode in the passion, which character would you stop? What questions would you ask?

Passion (Palm) Sunday
Year B

Isaiah 50:4–7 • Philippians 2:6–11 • Mark 14:1–15:47

Palm Sunday in Jerusalem begins at nightfall on Saturday. The weekly ritual of the ancient Jewish Sabbath has ended. Revelers return home from restaurants and theaters, noisy and exuberant, but in the Christian Quarter quiet and darkness await the dawn. The city walls, brilliantly illuminated a few hours ago, are now heavy with the night under a moon obscured by winter's last clouds. These walls hold tight in their clutches, in their protective darkness, the intrigues of the centuries. Jesus once said, "These very stones will shout," but tonight these massive monuments to human fear and ambition sit as silent sentinels awaiting the dawn.

Inside the walls Jerusalem's people sleep uneasily, mindful of the events that once took place here, aware of the ever-present dangers of the night—and of betrayals and of messiahs. The city squares are deserted, no children playing, no hawker peddling. Even the muezzin sleeps. Once in these streets the voice of Isaiah was heard announcing the birth of a messiah king. In these streets a joyous crowd proclaimed the Galilean rabbi their messiah. Nearby, down the hill, also in darkness, a cock continues to crow the betrayals of us all. In the darkness, the playground of thieves and the clothing of uneasy consciences and cowards, Jesus was arrested. While he prayed, he was arrested.

The name of the darkness is sin. And death. And you and me. We stumble in the darkness looking for the words that Peter couldn't find. When confronted with our betrayals and our fear of the dark, we run off naked before God, like the mysterious young man in today's account from Mark.

As the rising sun glistens above the Mount of Olives, Christians from Jerusalem and the nearby villages and from all over the world will begin the steep ascent to the town of Bethphage where they will begin to walk the ancient path that brought Jesus into Jerusalem, to Calvary, and to the resurrection. Along that public route private thoughts of faith and of betrayal, of following and of fleeing will fill every pilgrim searching for light, for Christ. Each will be reminded of the tendency to watch life safely from the sidelines, to watch others carry crosses, like the crowds that watch this annual spectacle rather than participate in it.

This forest of palm and olive branches advances through the winding street, down the slope of the Mount, past Gethsemane where disciples once slept off the Passover wine, up to the city gate that beckons us all to enter.

Here we come, we disciples of Jesus. Even though we may be far behind him, we follow our Lord, who is our way, not just a light from the past. Palm Sunday is not just a remembrance of the past, but a vivid reminder of the roles we live in the drama of faith today. Through the days of our lives we live many of the roles acted out in today's lengthy gospel. Some of them embarrass us, so strong is the truth they embody. Some of them challenge us, but most of all, from all the messiness of the passion they offer hope because we believe that the gospel does not end with darkness and the passion.

At the beginning of Mark's gospel we read, "Here begins the gospel of Jesus Christ, the Son of God." Throughout the entire gospel Mark leads up to the proclamation of the pagan centurion, "Truly this was the Son of God." Because we believe this, Palm Sunday and my life do not end in death, but with faith in God who conquers darkness and who will raise the crucified Jesus from the dead.

During this dangerous week we will wander around in the darkness, sometimes with Jesus, sometimes with the crowd. During this Holy Week we will be silent often. The sheer magnitude of all that we see and hear and remember about our faith is compacted into these days of awe.

Questions for Reflection

1. What darkness still hovers in my life, this close to Lent's end?

2. What light to others have I become because of my own lenten discipline?

3. Where can I put this year's palm in my home to remind me of this gospel and this week?

4. What time are the celebrations of the Lord's Supper and Good Friday and the Easter Vigil in my parish? Whom should I invite to join me in the observance?

5. Why is it always safer to be part of the crowd? When and how do I seek safety in the crowd?

Passion (Palm) Sunday
Year C

Luke 19:28–40 (Blessing of Palms) • Isaiah 50:4–7
Philippians 2:6–11 • Luke 22:14–23:56

These days the car trip from Galilee to Jerusalem takes about two hours. The road twists through the Jordan Valley, following the route of that famous river. In ancient times the journey was made by foot. Whole villages packed their duffel bags and trekked three times a year to Jerusalem for the great feasts of Succoth, Pentecost, and Passover. It took several days to cover the distance, even longer if one took the long route to avoid the perilous territory of the Samaritans.

Three times a year the people of Israel returned to Jerusalem and its magnificent Temple, as bidden by the law of God. Such a journey was never easy; it was always dangerous. Water was always in short supply. The roads were a series of tortuous, uphill hairpin curves. Bandits and wild animals lurked along the way. It still is dangerous. The danger, though, lies not so much in the wild beasts then or in political difficulties now. That would be easy. No, the danger lies in what Jerusalem does inside of people. Jerusalem makes us think. Jerusalem shows us the truth. Jerusalem stones prophets and crucifies messiahs.

That uphill road to Jerusalem is filled with stones. One would think that God scattered all the pebbles on earth here, to get inside pilgrims' sandals, to add irritation to the already difficult journey. Legend says that no one was allowed to enter this holy city with any kind of sorrow. The stones that line the way are the jettisoned sorrows of the pilgrims of the ages. So many stones! So many sorrows! So many Via Dolorosas, Ways of the Cross.

Luke's gospel portrays Jesus' life as a journey to Jerusalem.

In the reading for the blessing of palms, Jesus finally arrives at his destination, but Jerusalem will not be kind to him. Like all pilgrims, he enters from the Mount of Olives, which looms on the eastern border of the city, separating it from the wilderness. Many small villages still dot its landscape, like Bethpage and Bethany. Like all the other pilgrims, Jesus walks over the crest of the mountain and catches his first view of the Temple. The crowd of pilgrims always shouted for joy at the first glimpse of this place. "Blessed is he who comes in the name of the Lord!" This was their enthusiastic greeting to one another.

Jesus begins his entry to Jerusalem like any other pilgrim. But soon, as always with Jesus, things change. The words of honor are directed at him! Recognizing that Jesus has come to Jerusalem in God's name, the crowd shouts: "Hosanna!" (Please, save us!) In deference to this great one in their midst, they place their cloaks on the ground, a sign of respect. Notice that no palms are mentioned here. The people are using their very own clothing!

The pilgrim Jesus is acclaimed by the crowd, the same people who will shout for his death within the week. As Jesus makes his way down the slope, he passes the ancient cemeteries, an omen of what is to come. He goes past the garden where he will pray and where he could escape the treachery of Judas after the Last Supper. "Peace in heaven and glory in the highest!" sing the crowds, like the angels on Christmas night. Everything is coming full circle. So powerfully filled with God, acclaimed by the crowds, this is the same Jesus who will be emptied of everything, even of life, by week's end.

Everyone makes this journey to Jerusalem. With Jesus. For some, there are many sorrows that need to be dealt with and healed. For others, there will be the glance toward Peter, a nod from Jesus. Forgiveness. Understanding. Love. Some of us are like the thief, grabbing a final chance to steal heaven through someone else's goodness. Jesus understands that too. What matters is that we keep making the pilgrimage toward heaven and into our souls. What matters is that this journey through Lent never really stops, but that we keep on moving closer to God. Many things will happen to Jesus this week in Jerusalem. Celebration. Betrayal. Suffering. Death. Resurrection.

Whose footsteps will you follow this week? Peter's? Judas's? The crowd's? Or those of Jesus? What will Jerusalem do to you? What will Jerusalem do in you?

Questions for Reflection

1. What stone, what sorrow, needs to be jettisoned from your soul before Easter?

2. Has your lenten pilgrimage led you closer to Jesus? How?

3. Why would the crowd turn on Jesus? What do we learn from this "mob psychology"?

4. If you had to write a personal way of the cross, what would your betrayals be? Your trials? Who accuses you falsely? Who stands by you? Who helps you? Who judges you? What person you do judge? Whose crosses do you help carry? What hope remains in you, awaiting God's Easter call?

Monday of Holy Week

Isaiah 42:1–7 • Psalm 27 • John 12:1–11

Many were going over to Jesus and believing in him on account of Lazarus.

One book describes Lazarus as a pilgrim through time, someone that Jesus forgot. He roams the centuries waiting for the end of the world, waiting to be summoned by the same commanding voice that once called him forth from his tomb.

Another book describes Lazarus as a rather sickly fellow after his resuscitation. He was never quite the same again. The grave had done that to him, made him sallow, pale. When he was about to be captured by Jesus' enemies, he disappeared in a puff of dust when they laid hands on him. He had been there in some form, but not quite as a human.

What a fascinating fellow this Lazarus is! In literature and in theology, he captures our imaginations. Nowhere in the Bible does anyone ever ask him what it was like to be dead, what it was like to be brought back from death. The most understandable of all questions, those about dying and rising, remain unanswered in the Bible. Perhaps there is some comfort in this gospel where we read that Lazarus, evidently, could get hungry and eat at a banquet in Jesus' honor!

There is a reason for not knowing the answers to these death questions, of course. If we had the answers, we would no longer need faith. Faith means to trust, not to know; it means placing ourselves at the disposal of God, who does know. And who loves. In what Jesus did for Lazarus, the witnesses saw two kinds of love: the human love of a friend for a friend, and the divine love of God at work in Jesus. At both levels, people were made to think. Those whose thinking was holy came to understand. Thus, the statement: "Many were going over to Jesus and believing in him on account of Lazarus."

Even when Jesus was on his slow walk to the village of Bethany after the death of his friend Lazarus, he makes it clear that he tarried in order to make a point: He is the resurrection and the life.

It could be dangerous to believe this. The fact that "many were going over to Jesus and believing in him on account of Lazarus" raised the hackles of the ever-envious leaders. We saw that in our lenten gospels this last week. Jesus' words separate people into two camps: believers and scoffers. Scoffers try to take away faith; they steal trust. We know that they tried to stop John the Baptist. Our whole Holy Week drama is about what they tried to do to Jesus. In this gospel we see that they try to eliminate Lazarus as well. Clearly, it is dangerous to associate with this Jesus. If we identify with him, with his vision and way of looking at life, we threaten those who are always ready to settle for less, who are out only for themselves.

Perhaps that was Judas's problem. He figures in this gospel too. The other disciples must have known what sort of character he was. You cannot travel around with someone, as the apostles did, and not get to know him. Perhaps some even whispered the sad truth of Judas's thievery to Jesus. If they did, what could Jesus have thought? What could he have said to Judas? We don't know that either. We know only that Jesus kept Judas and called him friend, even at the moment of betrayal.

As we move into the mystery of this week, with all its power and pageantry, these readings set the tone. Isaiah reminds us to be servants of God, servants of the truth. The gospel reminds us that Jesus is the truth we serve. Sometimes we serve Jesus and his truth, as Martha and Mary did at the banquet. Sometimes we serve by being like Lazarus, trusting, even if we don't understand what God is doing to us or through us. Sometimes, too, we are like Judas: on the lookout for ourselves.

The humble village of Bethany still exists on the slopes of the Mount of Olives. So, too, do the Martha and Mary and Judas and Lazarus characters of this gospel. They continue to live in each of us. As we make our final week's journey into Lent, we hear these words and take the time to make sure that the Lazarus in us, the sign of Jesus' call to new life in us, is strong.

Lord God, the power of your goodness never ceases to amaze me. In this gospel, I see your goodness in Martha and Mary and Lazarus and Mary Magdalene, and I see my own treachery in Judas. Jesus called each of them "friend." As this Holy Week opens, help me to define my role in your plan. May I see what final service, like Mary Magdalene, I should do for your Son. May I also see, as Mary and Martha and Lazarus did, what final hospitality I can offer as I prepare for the ultimate hospitality of Holy Thursday. Lord, help me to make this week holy. Amen.

Tuesday of Holy Week

Isaiah 49:1–6 • Psalm 71 • John 13:21–33,36–38

It was night.

This is a week of intrigue and intensity. The intensity builds day after day toward Good Friday, then Easter Sunday. The intrigue reveals itself in each day's readings, all of them familiar to us, yet each tugging at us anew in a new Holy Week. New experiences, new disappointments, new sadness, and new hope always commingle to bring fresh insight into the meaning of this special week.

Today we see the intrigue of the disciples. Imagine the apostles' feeling of sharing the ancient Passover supper and learning that one of the group betrayed Jesus, and is, indeed, a traitor to all. Did they know Judas's character? Was the news really such a surprise? Yesterday's reading would indicate that they had a sense of his treachery. Perhaps they were all puzzled at Jesus for keeping him in the group all along.

We also see the humanity of the disciples: Peter signaling to John to ask Jesus who the traitor is; boasting Peter again put into his place. So much going on in such a short time!

The main characters in this gospel are the same ones who take the lead in Friday's passion story and in Sunday's account of the resurrection: Jesus, Peter, John, Judas. And somewhere in all of this, we can find ourselves again.

This episode begins with Judas's betrayal. Then a shared meal and words about following and not following Jesus. Finally, the episode ends in another kind of betrayal, that of Peter. We are always appalled at what Judas did, but how different was it from Peter's betrayal? From our own betrayals?

"It was night." John tells us that these betrayals, like the betrayal in the Garden of Gethsemane, all take place at night.

In John's gospel, light and darkness are always at war with each other, like good and evil in our souls. Danger always lurks in the darkness. No matter what century or what soul, night is the time that gives evil the upper hand.

This week leads us slowly but surely to the final darkness of Holy Saturday. It seemed to those first followers of Jesus that the power of night, the power of darkness and evil had won. But then comes the Easter Vigil. Then comes the light. At first, just a solitary pillar of light in the darkness. The servant of God is described that way in today's first reading: hidden at first, but then the glorious light of those who do God's will shines forth.

That is the movement of our Holy Week spirituality: from darkness to light, from evil to good, from betrayal to faith, from fear to confidence, from death to life.

Lord God, the power of darkness seems so strong. I know deep inside how your light and the world's darkness struggle for control of my soul. I realize too that sometimes I betray you. But in this Holy Week, I hear you speak to my heart and seek to be close to you, as John was, at the table of the Eucharist, at the table of your love, at the feast of forgiveness. During these sacred days, may I grow ever closer to you. Amen.

Wednesday of Holy Week

Isaiah 50:4–9 • Psalm 69 • Matthew 26:14–25

"Surely not I, Lord?"

For some time now I've wanted to reflect on a widespread problem today, being busy. I've never found quite the right passage to open up to the reflections that spin around in my mind. Today, of all days, I think I've found it!

For the third day in a row, our first reading is from the poetic faith of the prophet Isaiah. Scholars call this section of the book "Second Isaiah." His own deep faith spills out of his soul in beautiful words and profound thoughts. The passages offered for our reflection these days are called the "servant songs." The fourth of these will be heard on Good Friday. Each of them describes the ideal listener of God's word, a person whose life is dedicated to doing what is right, and in doing so pays a price. The servant songs describe a perfect response to God's initiatives, detailing how that servant spends a lifetime occupied with the work of God.

What a contrast today's gospel offers! Its central character is Judas Iscariot, the betrayer. We've caught glimpses of him in the other Holy Week readings. He is a thief who helps himself to the common purse. Disappointed in Jesus, he is also a betrayer. In this passage from Matthew, we see a very busy Judas. Doing what? The disciples are preparing the Passover Supper for Jesus. Because this special meal of the Jews demanded a lot of preparation, special foods and arrangements all had to be made. As twilight sets in on Passover night, households and cities come to a standstill. The only thing worth doing at this eveningtide is renewing the ancient Seder, or Passover, ceremony. That is what Judas should have been busy doing.

Christian tradition places this supper on Mount Sion. This gospel tells us that Judas was elsewhere, across the city where the chief priests could be found. Never mind that they too should have been busy about the work of God. They are busy, instead, with secret, evil schemes—hardly the work of God's servants.

From there Judas had to cross the city again, through the streets crowded with last-minute shoppers, tourists, and pilgrims. Even in those days. Back to Mount Sion, running back and forth, to and fro. There's Judas! Does this begin to sound familiar?

Once he has returned to the dinner table, to the Upper Room, he doesn't stay long. He asks his question, "Surely not I, Lord?" knowing well the answer. Did his manner betray what he was about to do? Was he out of breath? Acting odd? Was he attentive to the prayers of the ritual, or was his mind elsewhere, plotting the evening's iniquity?

How often are we so busy that our minds and spirits seem split in two? Mental busy-ness. Spiritual busy-ness. Physical busy-ness. Look at what we do to our lives! In the process, look what we do to ourselves! Does all this busy-ness describe us? Does it define us? "Surely not I, Lord," who am too busy?

Judas isn't finished. He must still leave the dinner table, cross the city again to the Roman garrison, then lead them out of the city, across the Kidron Valley to the Garden of Gethsemane for his act of treachery. This is a busy man!

I don't know of a single instance in the Bible where it says we should be so busy in our daily lives. Jesus never seemed that occupied! Quite the opposite! He always took "alone time" to reflect and pray. Even on the night of his betrayal, when he might have been busy making escape plans, he goes out to pray. There is a lesson here for us, isn't there?

We are human be-ings, not human do-ers. As Lent closes, we need to look back over the days and weeks of Lent and see if we have been faithful to our Ash Wednesday promises. Or have we been too busy to pray? Too busy to do charity? Too busy to fast from being occupied every minute of our day? Being busy is not a virtue; I am convinced of that. Even children imitate us, going from activity to activity and whining of boredom the moment they must sit still. We train them to be busy. We even make ourselves busier by carting them around to all their activities!

Judas was a busy man, wasn't he? Lent calls us to slow our lives down, to make time and space for Jesus in our lives so that at our Easter Vigil we can genuinely renew our baptismal promises. We should be "new" ourselves because we have taken time to let God's grace re-create us. Or are we too busy?

Busy Judas or the prayerful servant of God? Which are you?

Lord God, you once scolded Martha for being too busy. Today I see the result of all that activity: betrayal. Help me to slow down the sounds of all my "machines"— whatever keeps me busy—and the beating of my heart so that I can relax into your Word and into your love and recline at the banquet you offer us: words to live by, food to share. Make me more and more your servant, attentive to you and to others, less concerned about the clock and myself. Amen.

Holy Thursday

Exodus 12:1–8,11–14 • 1 Corinthians 11:23–26
John 13:1–15

A loaf of bread. A jug of wine. Entrance is free. These are essential elements of our Holy Thursday liturgy. This perhaps doesn't ring in our ears as something profound or spectacular; in fact, the opposite is almost true. It sounds very ordinary. But then, look at the words more carefully. Listen to them again. Bread. Wine. These are the staples of life. Bread to nourish the body, wine to quench our thirst. Without them, we soon perish. They are the food of common people—our food.

But there is something different: the third element, the entrance fee. There is none. No charge for this bread or wine. No restaurant does this. No grocer gives away food. No parent charges their children a table fee to eat dinner. Neither does our God. Here we are, the people of God, gathering to eat and drink. No entrance charge at the door. This is the family meal of the people of God.

It is also a mysterious meal. The mystery lies not in the common ingredients of wheat and grape, but in this: the origin of the meal is in sacrifice. In our time so many families no longer share a meal together. Schedules and activities rob us of sitting down at table and sharing hopes and problems and needs and plans. No wonder this sacred meal confuses people. Fast food robs us of seeing the work, the sacrifice of preparing the food that gives us life. With this sacred meal, there is no fast food. There is only eternity. "This is the cup of my blood of the new and everlasting covenant."

It is a dangerous meal, this free meal. It is dangerous precisely because it is free. Belief in this meal threatens the world that loves to charge for bread and wine. It is dangerous because of its price: the life of Jesus, the Son of God. It is dangerous because in this meal everyone who shares the bread and drinks from the cup is making a pledge to love one another and God.

Eating this meal celebrates our freedom: from sin, from death, and freedom from those who would control and manipulate us for their personal gain. This meal celebrates freedom from every kind of slavery. All who share the meal are equal at this table. This meal subverts the values of the world. That is why the world tries to make fun of it and tries to lure away those who believe in its power and its mystery.

In the gospel of this evening we hear about Jesus continuing to do what is dangerous. It was dangerous because it reversed reality and turned the thinking of the world upside down. Before sharing the meal, he washed the feet of his followers. Jesus, the teacher, washed the feet of his students. Jesus, the Son of God, washed the feet of the Father's creation. This was the work of slaves, not of householders, and certainly not of gods. Peter understood this and protested. It was not embarrassment that provoked Peter to say, "Lord, do you wash my feet?" It was hard reality; Peter understood exactly what was happening; nothing would ever be the same again. God was at work in Jesus—serving people. The great inequality between God and people, between teacher and student, is wiped away when Jesus stooped to wash feet.

The message is eminently clear: we must do the same. Not to do this is to prefer the way of the world, to dominate other people, militarily, physically, emotionally, economically, spiritually. Jesus will have no part in this. Only friendship, characterized by service to all, reflects the will of God who becomes a servant in Jesus and in us.

On this night of all nights, when we read of the great liberation of the Hebrews from slavery at the hands of the Egyptians, we also read about the freedom Jesus earns for us by his death. This freedom, Jesus insists, we must bestow generously to one another: husband and wife, children and parents, neighbor and neighbor, teacher and student, priest and people, stranger and stranger.

Among the people who share the bread and who drink the wine there are only equals. There is no rank. That is dangerous talk in the ears of the world. In the family of God, father and son are equal. Wife and husband are equal. Superior and inferior cease to exist. Male and female are equal. Leader and follower are equal. Friendship and faith make the categories of the world, the divisions of rank, irrelevant. All are equal and all are free because all share the same bread and the same cup and the same friendship with Jesus, who washes feet.

This is hard to comprehend, so Jesus asks "Do you understand what I have done to you?" Parishes exist so that those who believe can nourish themselves on the bread and wine and by serving one another. They exist, also, to help carry the inevitable crosses of tomorrow's Good Friday. To only eat and drink is not enough. If we come forward for the meal, it cannot be only because it is free. It must be to strengthen ourselves for the service we are called to give. It must give us strength to carry crosses for one another. "Do you understand what I have done to you?" Do you understand what I have done? Do you understand?

Questions for Reflection

1. In our world, we like to think of ourselves as democratically equal. In what ways does the gospel of Jesus tell us we are equal?

2. The Passover Meal celebrated the freedom of the Hebrews. How does our every sharing in this meal confirm our freedom in Jesus?

3. The Washing of Feet cannot be only a ritual. In what ways do you, should you, wash the feet of others?

4. It may be clear how the sacrificial meal of the Eucharist and the sacrifice on the cross are related to each other. How are the washing of feet and the sacrifice of the cross related to each other?

Good Friday

Isaiah 52:13–53:12 • Hebrews 4:14–16,5:7–9
John 18:1–19:42

It is Good Friday, one of the holiest days of the year. And one of the strangest, one of the most unusual. There are several reasons for this: It is a Friday, and many Christians go to church, not where people usually are on Friday afternoons. There are people in church today we do not usually see at worship with us. That too makes it unusual. The element that makes it most unusual—most special, and therefore holy—is that much of the business world closes down for a few afternoon hours. For just a little while, worship of God surpasses the need for money.

We are inclined today to focus on the more familiar reading of the passion of Jesus. But it is impossible to understand these final acts of Jesus without understanding the background, to understand things the way Jesus did. In the first reading, from Isaiah, we read this: "Through his suffering my servant shall justify many, and their guilt he shall bear." This role of suffering for others is the very opposite of what the world teaches. In the words of Isaiah there is no self-assertion. There is no claim to "my rights." There is only willingness to suffer for others and submission to the will of God.

The beginning of the reading says, "See, this is my servant." We are not a people who think first of serving others. We look down on those who serve others and we consider them inferior. The purely human interpretation of the world looks after the self first. It is as simple as that. I am number one; others come second, at best. To place oneself, much less one's life, at the service of others, is simply viewed as foolish by the world, which tells us that money, power, position, and self are more important than integrity and sacrifice for others.

Because Jesus believed in the values of integrity and sacrifice—so threatening to the world—he had to die. Christianity is always caught somewhere between the world in which we live, with its values and its ways, and this world of Jesus.

Good Friday is not just the memory of what happened long ago. It is the reality of what is happening all around us, all the time. When we observe the sufferings of others, we should understand that they are not being punished for their sins, but are paying the price for sin in the world, for our sins. Our children play with their food at school, while most children in the world go hungry. Our cup of coffee is cheap because of the near-slave labor of Third World peasants. The anguish of people around the world who only hope for shelter cries out to God more loudly than our complaints. The fear of Palestinian mothers whose children might not come home from school one day drowns out the whines of our students who protest they have too much homework. The *campesino* with no medicine has needs far greater than the pill-laden hypochondriac. And so on. And so on.

Jesus offered himself as a victim so that we would not have to be victims ourselves. This Jesus paid the price for our sins so that we would not have to. Wherever there is undeserved suffering, those people are also, like Jesus, servants. They are the unnamed poor and powerless of the world who pay for our comforts and for our successes and for our well-being, just as Jesus paid for our eternal life.

No person's suffering is trivial, without purpose. No human death goes unnoticed by God. All this is because of Good Friday, when Jesus, the Son of God, experienced the ultimate human suffering: death.

There will always be people who do not care about God, or Jesus, or us. There will always be those who will choose not to observe Good Friday, or any other religious feast. What matters is that we understand Good Friday. As we hear the words of these readings and reverence the body of Jesus on the cross, then we are saying that we are willing to do what Jesus did: to go the distance for others. In a society that takes a dim view of any inconvenience, much less of any sacrifice, in a society that cannot take no for an answer, the words of Isaiah are in danger of being lost. And the death of Jesus on the cross is in danger of being trivialized, of becoming nothing more than an ornament of gold around someone's neck.

Crosses and Good Friday go together. They have meaning for those who believe. They tell us that God is on our side, that God understands. They also ask the hard question, every Good Friday, every day: Do you understand?

Questions for Reflection

1. Is it good or not so good that crosses have become decoration, jewelry for people?

2. How do we treat those who serve us, or wait on us?

3. How does today's observance relate to yesterday's Last Supper? To tomorrow's Easter Vigil?

4. What sacrifices have I made in Lent that can be offered in a new way today?

5. Why is it dangerous to let Good Friday only become an observance of what happened long ago and to overlook the ways Good Friday is taking place around us today?

Easter Sunday

Acts 10:34,37–43 • Colossians 3:1–4 • John 20:1–9

Every day I lived in Jerusalem I walked past the Church of the Holy Sepulchre. Inside, pilgrims jostled one another and priests of various rites competed with one another's prayers in order to raise a louder voice to God. In our Roman Rite, only the Mass of Easter is celebrated in this church. Every day is Easter here. The pilgrims, often disappointed by the dark and dank interior of the stone building, are all drawn to one place. No matter which rite is being celebrated, no matter what language is used, all stand in line to enter the monument that marks the place where the body of Jesus was laid. All wait to enter the empty tomb, to see the nothingness that is the sacrament of resurrection.

Today's gospel recalls the first witnesses to Christ's resurrection. In the early hours of the post-Passover dawn a courageous, solitary woman, Mary Magdalene, made her way through the streets of Jerusalem to perform a final act of love for Jesus, to come to the tomb that the others, who had run away, had never seen. She would make her way past the shopkeepers, eager to open up after the Passover closing, and past the soldiers who patrolled the streets. To get to the tomb, in those days, she had to leave the protection of the city walls and go to this cemetery of caves in an abandoned rock quarry. Once safely there, she saw . . . only an empty tomb. What could it mean? What could have happened to Jesus?

Next John and Peter came along in haste, past the same shops, past the same early morning crowds, past the same soldiers they so feared on Good Friday. They too look in and see nothing. No body rests there, only the clothing of the grave. John peers into the empty tomb, and, like Mary Magdalene, sees nothing. But he believes. The empty tomb confirmed for

John that Jesus was right: death could not contain him; he was risen from the dead. Death would never be the same again. The world would never be the same again. Today we make that same journey to the tomb of Jesus, each in a different way. Some of us see the empty tomb and understand. Others see only emptiness.

For most of us, the period between Good Friday and Easter Sunday lasts much longer than three days. Doubts about our lives and our world, fear of the future and of sickness, pain, and dying, preoccupation with the trials of our own lives often make Jesus' trial and death seem long ago and far away. The contrast between our noisy world and the quiet of the tomb can overwhelm us. But Jesus doesn't let us stay overwhelmed, any more than he remained dead.

What does this empty tomb mean? What can we learn at Easter? We learned on Good Friday that all of us, even the Son of God, must die. Good Friday also teaches us that without Jesus our lives are empty and our world is lost. But Easter teaches us the same lesson it taught Mary Magdalene and Peter and John: Jesus did not cease to exist. He is alive; he is with us. We can turn to him in our doubts and he will calm us. Jesus is more alive than ever, waiting for us to come to the tomb, to search for him each day in the reality of human existence.

Jesus trusted in God's power to raise him up. So do we. Easter faith teaches us that only fools look into the empty tomb and see nothing. We look into the empty tomb and see our faith vindicated. This Jesus who was dead is alive. We who were dead to sin are alive in Jesus, who has loosened death's grip on our souls and on our world. The empty tomb that is our soul can be filled with God's gracious power to save us, even from sin and death.

Mary, Peter, and John sang no Alleluias at their discovery. In quick silence they returned to their friends and told them what had happened. In awe and wonder they came to under-

164

stand all that Jesus had done, all that he had said. His promise to them came to pass, as it will for all of us who make the pilgrimage through life: first suffering, then new life. First, Good Friday, then Easter Sunday. First death, then resurrection. It is the pattern set for all time in Jesus.

Questions for Reflection

1. What new life has come to you as a result of Lent and Easter?

2. What questions or fears still linger in your mind about death? About rising?

3. Easter is celebrated with many symbols. Which one is your favorite? Why?

4. Pope John Paul II recently called our world "a culture of death." In what ways do his words reflect our cultural preoccupation with death? In what ways do these words continue the message of Jesus about life and new life?

5. Why doesn't the world which once crucified Jesus want him to be alive?

6. What are the signs of new life in you? In your family? Your neighborhood? Your parish?

Of Related Interest ...

If They Could Speak
Ten Witnesses to the Passion of Jesus
John D. Powers
"Voices" from the past including those of James, Judas, Pilate, Mary Magdalene, Mary, Christ's Mother and others come into our time to reveal truths about Jesus.

ISBN: 0-89622-421-X, 64 pp, $4.95 (order C-25)

The Parables of Calvary
Reflections on the Seven Last Words of Jesus
Stephen C. Rowan
The author examines the seven brief phrases, or "words," uttered by Jesus as he lay dying on the cross.

ISBN: 0-89622-576-3, 48 pp, $4.95 (order B-77)

Still on the Cross
Meditations on the Human Condition and the Desperate Passion of Jesus
Loretta Girzaitis & Richard L. Wood
Links the passion of Christ with contemporary injustice and highlights the Christian mission to continue Christ's saving work.
ISBN: 0-89622-449-X, 80 pp, $5.95 (order W-32)

In Joyful Expectation
Advent Prayers and Reflections
Laurin Wenig
The daily prayers and reflections found in this book use the Scripture readings for Advent to challenge readers to find Christ amid the solitude and longing that characterize the season.

ISBN: 0-89622-596-8, 112 pp, $7.95 (order M-01)

Available at religious bookstores or from

XXIII TWENTY-THIRD PUBLICATIONS
P.O. Box 180 • Mystic, CT 06355 • 1-800-321-0411